COUNTRY WISE

COUNTRY WISE

Phil Drabble

Michael Joseph – London

First published in Great Britain by Michael Joseph Ltd
44 Bedford Square, London WC1
1980

ISBN 0 7181 1952 5

Photoset in Great Britain by
D. P. Media Limited, Hitchin, Hertfordshire.
Printed by Hollen Street Press Ltd, Slough, Berkshire
and bound by Dorstel Press Ltd, Harlow, Essex

Contents

List of Illustrations

Acknowledgements

The author and publisher would like to thank the following for permission to reproduce the photographs in this book: the folios refer to the chapter in which the photographs appear.

Stanley Porter: 1, 8, 14, 26, 28, 29, 33, 41, 43, 52
Derek Johnson: 3, 12, 16, 35, 49
S. C. Brown: 4
John Humphreys: 6
Dave Parfitt: 10, 20, 54
E. D. Lewis: 18
Netherfield Visual Productions: 22
Robin Williams: 24, 31
Michael Clarke: 44
John Tarlton: 46
P. Bennett: 50
David Tomlinson: 56
Anne Jordan: 57
R. P. Lawrence: 59
W. Wilkinson: 60

Author's Foreword

Although I served a 'life sentence', working in a factory in the Black Country of Staffordshire before escaping to earn my living with my pen, I enjoyed every minute of it. Indeed, I have enjoyed every period of my life even better than the period before because I have mixed in the melting pot with so many charming people.

Most Black Countrymen, and I am proud to be numbered amongst them, are no more than two generations from ancestors who earned their living on the land but were forced by circumstances to drift into the towns by the Industrial Revolution. I benefited from this inherited love of country things by growing up with patients of my father – a Black Country doctor with a mining practice which included the no-man's-land between industry and lovely countryside that strangers can't believe can be found in central Staffordshire. Miners are traditionally among the best poachers and they taught me the tricks of their trade that are mysteries beyond the ken of academic school gaffers.

So I grew up with a love of country things that was uncluttered from the prejudices that too often divide Town from Country and can get as much pleasure from a Sunday morning's ferreting for rats or rabbits as I can from watching rare birds from binoculars or enjoying the beauty of wild flowers.

I yearned to escape the factory life as much because I wanted to be my own boss as because of my longing for the solitudes of quiet places. At the age of forty-seven I changed courses and, for the past nineteen years, I have been working for myself, earning my living with my pen, writing and broadcasting about natural history and country topics. In 1964, I bought a cottage and ninety acres of woodland which I have since managed as a wildlife reserve.

While still in industry, I had written various articles for the Birmingham *Evening Mail* and, when he heard that I intended to manage my land as a wildlife reserve, the editor invited me to share the experience with regular readers under the title of 'Goat Lodge Diary'. Three years later he suggested that I widen the brief to do a series called 'Country Scene', with a natural history bias but ranging wider than the restrictions of my own boundaries. In 1976, he invited me to take a wider brief, under the title 'Phil Drabble', and in this column I am free to write about my own reserve and how it developed or to range where I like throughout the countryside.

This book is a selection from these weekly columns, chosen by my publisher, to follow two earlier books, *Country Scene* and *Country Seasons* chosen from the same source, all with the permission of the Editor of the *Evening Mail*.

I have tilted at windmills in my efforts to help obtain protection for threatened otters and spoken my mind about the sportsmen who bait badgers and the scientists who persecute them equally cruelly usually on circumstantial evidence. But most of the book is not about the dangers of chemical pesticides or the iniquities of those who threaten our wildlife. It is about the pleasant people and animals and birds with whom I am lucky enough to share my life.

1. An Osprey Off Course

A fringe benefit of being a naturalist is that strangers often unload their waifs and strays on me. Orphaned hares and injured badgers, found-ling birds and stray deer, have all had the Freedom of my Wood conferred upon them. But the most distinguished visitor arrived one day when I was out.

My wife says he had a wicked gleam in his yellow eye and his cruel hooked bill looked capable of murder. At the risk of being called a name-dropper, I must tell you he was an osprey.

Now ospreys are fish eagles, only glimpsed occasionally as rare passage migrants in the Midlands. This one was unusually late in the

The male osprey brings sticks for the nest at Loch Garten, while the female looks on.

season. Ospreys are sometimes in the news when irresponsible louts rob eggs from under the noses of wardens guarding known nests in Scotland for the Royal Society for the Protection of Birds.

The bird came to our house under escort. A local bird watcher had been having the thrill of his life watching him hunting fish in a nearby reservoir. Although he was so rare, there was no mistaking him because he had the distinguished white head of a fish eagle, was dark brown above with white under-parts and a wing span of more than four feet.

The bird watcher had watched him fly about fifty feet above the water, check and hover in mid-flight and drop like a stone with talons out-stretched. A second later, he reappeared grasping a fine rainbow trout in his greedy talons and flapped heavily to a pier of the bridge across the reservoir.

His witness didn't move a muscle for fear of disturbing him, but the fish was not played out. With a last convulsion, it slipped from its captor's grasp and slithered back into the water. The great bird swooped in anger from his perch and wheeled over the parapet to get a better view – at the precise moment when a car was speeding past.

The hawk never had a chance. The car's roof rack hit him and he somersaulted to earth in a puff of feathers to lie in peril of certain death from the next car to come along. The bird watcher scooped up the battered remains to discover the victim was bruised and stunned, but still alive. So he brought him to our house to see if there was anything I could do.

As I was out, my wife asked him to take the injured bird straight to the vet. Country vets are used to horses kicking and the flailing horns of angry bulls but, like me, few of them have been lucky enough to be introduced to a live osprey.

He eyed his patient warily and decided that, although he was still groggy, his powerful hooked bill looked capable of amputating a finger. He under-rated the talons, however, and discovered to his cost that shaking hands with an osprey was worse than picking up a handful of red-hot needles!

A superficial diagnosis suggested the bird was shocked and bruised, but nothing worse, so there seemed no reason why he should not recover with normal care. He telephoned the RSPB who sent their local warden to collect him to see if he was fit to be sent to Scotland for release.

Next day he obviously felt better and had regained his proud arrogance, resentful of his captivity and savage with promise of the havoc he would wreak on anyone foolhardy enough to take liberties with him. So the warden released him from the RSPB reserve. The bird flew off but the area is hilly and wooded and not the sort of country where ospreys could easily find fish. There are reservoirs within a few miles which he may have been lucky enough to discover, but I should have felt happier if he had been fed on fish for a few days before release. Then he could have been set free from the reservoir where he had first been seen. The risk of being hit by another car seems less than the risk of turning him adrift where fish would be harder to catch.

At best, the odds against survival of such birds are great. They were extinct as a breeding species in Britain for many years because their diet of fish localised them to the very areas where sportsmen paid hard cash for fishing. The hawks brought the prey they captured to eat on the bank and it was standard practice to destroy any 'vermin' which threatened a salmon, trout or pheasant.

2.   Things That Go Bang In The Night

Every two or three minutes the air outside my window shivers and splits with an explosion of sound. The noise is not as sharp as shotgun fire nor as menacing as thunder when lightning strikes a tree. But it is very loud and happens so regularly that I have timed the intervals of silence with a stop-watch. I can now predict that the next bang will shatter my peace exactly two minutes and forty-three seconds later.

If my grandfather had been roused from sleep by such a din, he would have grabbed his cudgel and sallied forth with venom in his heart.

Things have changed since then. Such detonations are now as much seasonal rural sounds as the hum of combine harvesters or the whine of corn driers.

This fusillade which interrupts my tape-recordings stems from an automatic bird scarer, set to deter feathered raiders from a local field of newly-sown corn. Like so much else in the country, even bird scaring has been mechanised.

When I was a kid, farmers paid lads a tanner a day to walk round the fields with a pair of wooden clappers. They stalked up as close as they could to a raiding flock of birds and banged their clappers with the frenzy of a cymbals player. Wages have escalated since then so that it is now cheaper to buy a mechanical gadget that will work all hours without asking for overtime payment.

The modern bird scarer that obtrudes on me looks like an oversized blunderbuss, painted in brash and tasteless colours. It isn't loaded with powder and shot but emits a succession of loud bangs, powered by the same compressed gas that fuels heat and light for caravans and cookers.

In theory, it is illegal to allow it to go on banging at night but farmers are not noted for their addiction to theory! It is often easier to let it bang away than to walk down the fields to turn it off. And, because country folk are not moaners, nobody complains.

I harbour deep doubts about the effectiveness of such devices, though. Wildlife soon grows accustomed to mechanical noise and movement. Belfast airport, for example, is famous for its hares. No animal is more timid than a hare but vast numbers of them graze contentedly within a few yards of the runway used by snarling jet aircraft. These shy creatures have learned that they are neither coursed by dogs nor shot by men because airport security prevents either having access. So the hares are prepared to put up with the ear-splitting din in exchange for a secure place to feed.

With this in mind, I have monitored the reactions of our own wildlife to the bird scarer a field or so away. It so happened that the first time I heard it a party of four fallow deer were grazing in an open field. They were silhouetted against the green turf one second – and had melted like shadows into deep cover the next. They made no hustle, which might have attracted attention. They slid away as smoothly as a professional conjuring trick. Next day, they casually raised their heads and pricked their ears when they heard the same bang. The day after that they didn't even raise their heads.

The wild duck on our pool were a bit more scary. They have good reason to be because the shooting season has recently started. One of the saddest sights of autumn is to see the 'limpers' which return home to my pool after they have been wounded by some lout who took a pot-shot out of lethal range. They come hobbling up the paddock to feed on the fowl corn but, more often than not, a fox has them before they recover, or the wound proves mortal and they die a lingering death.

But even they soon learned the difference between sporting guns and the harmless scarer that was all bark and no bite.

Wood pigeons and rooks were probably the most likely robbers of the new corn so I wandered over to the field to watch the results of the banger's virtuoso performances at first hand. Flocks of birds were feeding and when the explosion shattered the silence, they rose in a cloud, circled round – and settled down again.

You can't catch old birds with chaff – and you can't scare them off for long with empty threats. A lad with a pair of clappers might cost more in wages, but he would have annoyed the birds more and me less.

3. My Deer Friend

The latest waif to land on our doorstep is a tiny muntjac deer, no bigger than a half-grown cat. A friend who owns a wildlife reserve in the Lake District telephoned to say that 'Munty' had been born on New Year's Day. His chances of survival in deep snow and bitter weather were so slim that she had rescued him and was bottle-rearing him in the bathroom. She wondered if I would like him.

Needing no second invitation, I collected him and now he is comfortably asleep by the radiator in my study. Tick, my sweet-natured pointer, has taken him under her wing. She nuzzles him with delight when I give him his bottle, four times a day. Then she licks his coat until she convinces herself that even his own mother couldn't have put a better shine of health on it. And she is unbelievably patient when he jumps on her in play – his tiny cloven hooves are as sharp as stiletto heels!

At present, his headquarters is a straw bed under the shelf in my study where I keep my tape-recording equipment. It is a shallow drawer, the same size as the shelf, with a plastic base to make it waterproof, and layers of absorbent newspaper in the interests of hygiene.

As things are turning out, this seems to be an unnecessary precaution. Muntjac deer are remarkable in many ways, not the least of which is their instinct for cleanliness. In the wild, they naturally leave their droppings in one area, so I take him into an outbuilding each time he has his bottle, and he has selected one corner as his private loo. When he has used it, I bring him back into the house where he is proving far easier to 'house train' than most dogs.

I have discovered over the years that deer are immensely rewarding to hand-rear because they seem to stay tame for the rest of their lives when allowed their complete freedom.

My first attempt was almost twenty years ago with Miss Roedoe, a roe deer which I bottle-reared and which lived to delight us for the next ten years. When she died, I reared Honey, my white fallow deer, and

16

Tick pays close attention during Jac's feeding time.

she is proving even more successful. Not only does she enjoy complete freedom in the wood, but she has had five fawns by wild bucks from the herd which she has joined.

She is a greedy old thing and still comes mincing out of the wood to meet me when she hears the rattle of my corn bucket. Her sense of security must be contagious because she brings her wild friends with her to share the food I put out on the bird table by the window. I am hoping that one day Munty will join a wild doe in the enclosure by the house to start a family of muntjac deer to join the other wild deer which live in the wood.

Muntjac are the smallest deer found in this country, for they are little bigger than a fox when full grown. They are also very noisy little creatures, with harsh staccato voices which have earned them the name 'Barking Deer'. The bucks have short antlers, rather like nanny-goat horns except that they 'cast' or shed them every year, as other deer do, after which they grow another set. Their most unusual feature is that they have a set of canine tushes, or teeth, in the upper jaw which are an effective defence!

Although fossil muntjac remains over 35,000,000 years old have been found, they didn't arrive in England until less than a century ago. The original stock was imported from China by a Duke of Bedford who also imported grey squirrels, the destructive tree rats which have ousted our more beautiful and harmless red squirrel. After a while, some of the Duke's muntjacs escaped from his walled park and have been spreading over the country ever since.

They feed on bramble, ivy and other broad-leaved plants, as well as grass, and they spread a few miles further through standing corn and hay and thick hedgerows every year. Because they are so tiny and secretive, they do very well in the large, neglected, over-grown gardens on the edges of big towns.

There are now wild muntjac in most of the southern counties and they are quite common in Warwickshire, south of Birmingham. But the conurbation of Birmingham and the Black Country seems to act as a barrier so that they are uncommon in Staffordshire and counties to the north. A few that got lost and blundered into building areas have been rescued and ended up in our wood, but they are so shy that we only see them rarely.

So I am delighted at the chance to hand-rear Munty because with luck, he will grow up tame and regard our house as 'home'. Then, when we introduce him to a mate, and his wild fellows meet up with him, he may persuade them to stay around so that they, too, may delight us by allowing us to observe them living free and happy in our wood.

4. Herons Harbinger The Spring

The herons came back, bang on St Valentine's day. A large colony nests in our wood each year and they have dispersed and gone by the end of August when the last of the season's young have learned to fly.

This is a wise precaution. In spite of the Protection of Birds Act, which makes them safe in theory, no insurance broker in his senses would issue a Life Policy on them. There are still too many trigger-happy Harrys who are never satisfied unless they are killing something. Herons are large and tempting targets for such vandals.

They are such noisy birds that the wood seems unnaturally silent when they are not there. Although they don't start nesting in earnest until the middle of February, we reckon to see the first birds of the season long before that. One of our annual treats is when the first scout calls round to check that all is well, usually on Christmas Day or Boxing Day. He circles the wood a time or two and then settles down to screech from the tree top that our heronry is still a desirable residence. Then he flies away.

When the weather is fine, from New Year onwards, increasing numbers fly in to roost. Each cock bird selects the nest he hopes his mate will use and the air echoes with their melancholy cries. From time to time, two birds will dispute possession of the same nest.

It is obvious that if their cries could be translated, they would bring blushes to the cheeks of tougher men than me. Strangers who stay the night are often convinced that the wood is haunted or that they are hearing the last screams of the victim of murder.

A spell of hard weather dampens their ardour so that the colony disperses, leaving the wood to its silence again until another breath of spring rekindles their desire.

This winter, we have been opening up a patch of wood at the edge of the heronry. We have grubbed out hazel nut bushes and burned them on bonfires. All the birch trees over a couple of acres have been felled and sawn into logs for the fire, leaving only the oak trees to stand.

My purpose was to see further into the wood and to let in more daylight. I hope this will encourage blackberry and wild rose to flourish, and provide extra fodder for the deer. It will also allow us to see much more of what is going on.

The snag is that you can't do work like that in silence. For several weeks, the air has been hideous with the destructive wail of chain-saws. Wildlife quickly grows accustomed to mechanical noise, and the deer were soon feeding within fifty yards of the racket the woodmen made. But I did wonder if it had scared the herons, although I had not spotted any near enough to hear it.

The arrival of their advance party has set my mind at rest, because we regard them as one of our success stories. Since we have been at

Herons at the nest: a youngster can just be seen.

Goat Lodge, the colony has increased from fourteen nests to fifty-five, largely because we never disturb them or allow anyone else to do so. So far, only ten have arrived this year. This is not as depressing as it might seem because the latecomers every year are about six weeks after the first have gone to nest.

It is a wonderful hedge against disaster. We often get a late spell of snow or torrential rain or ice after the first clutch of eggs have been laid. Then the eggs get chilled and the chicks can die inside them before they can hatch. If all the birds had laid at the same time, it could have wiped out the whole year's crop of young. But last year's young, nesting for the first time, are anything up to six weeks behind the old birds so a spell of harsh weather does not wipe out the lot.

There were exceptionally good results last year and we haven't had prolonged hard weather so a high proportion should have survived. The next few weeks will prove – or disprove – the theory. With luck, each moonlit night should be more raucous than the last. By day, each huge untidy nest should sprout a motionless grey sentry bird.

The disturbance in the wood is now finished and even I shall not trespass into 'their' part of the wood until the young are past the vulnerable stage. I'll count the nests in May. By then I hope to hear the insatiable clamour of sturdy chicks and to see a shuttle service of great grey birds flying backwards and forwards to feed them.

5.   Tell The Froggies To Take A Jump

Common Market bureaucrats want to change our ways of exporting venison. They want us to plunge all our deer carcases into deep freeze within forty-eight hours of slaughter. That is change, but not improvement. I dread the thought that busybodies this side of the Channel will ape the idea and insist that we, too, eat game before it is properly hung.

Venison is the meat of red, roe or fallow deer which does not only need skilled cooking to come to the table at its best. It also has to be prepared by being hung for the right time, under the right conditions. If it has not been properly 'ripened', it has the texture of cotton wool and little more taste. Then it needs garlic and all the artificial sauces with which foreigners disguise the lack of flavour in the mush they serve.

I love simple, English food and venison is one of my favourite dishes. The meat needs hanging in a cold airy game larder for a week or ten days before anyone shows it the oven. This helps tenderise it and it imparts the wonderful flavour that distinguishes game from other meat.

Those who do not appreciate such niceties imagine that eating ripe game is like eating meat that has gone bad. It is certainly true that a calf or lamb allowed to hang as long as a pheasant, hare or deer would not only be unpleasant but possibly dangerous as well. The flesh would smell foul and become slimy and objectionable.

I once tried to discover what made some meats safe to hang as game while others would have 'gone off' and decayed under the same treatment. It occurred to me that the Jews had probably forgotten more than modern scientists know because I remembered whole chapters in the Old Testament devoted to the subject of 'clean' and 'unclean' meat.

I know that Jews don't eat pork and rabbit and my father, who was a doctor, once told me that none of his Jewish patients ever contracted some diseases common with other patients. His theory was that the list of unclean meats had been drawn up with the warm Mediterranean climate of Biblical days in mind. He thought the reason it was forbidden to eat certain meats was probably that they would have been the first to putrefy in the heat. The religious laws, therefore, would also have a highly practical purpose.

I tested his theory by telephoning a Rabbi and putting the question to him, but I soon got a dusty answer. I was told that unclean meat was unclean simply because it has been so described by the founders of the faith and that it had nothing to do with hygiene. Since most religious doctrine has a severely practical undertone for the good of society, I was surprised.

Deciding to try the other end of the scale, I asked the Public Health Department. The chap in charge of the inspectors who checked all meat killed in a chain of public abattoirs tried to blind me with science. He rabbited on with theories about changing enzymes and bacteria but he was soon stumped by a few basic questions about why his theories applied to meat but seemed to be confounded when applied to game.

The plain fact soon emerged that he didn't know why it was not only safe but pleasant to eat some meat when it was 'high' enough to be theoretically dangerous. As so often happens, it took a practical man to confound the boffins.

A family butcher friend came to my rescue: he knew and took for granted facts that do not seem to appear in the syllabus of hygiene or religious subjects. The first point he made was that all meats need some ripening. The factors that control how much are the age of the animal, whether it is fat or lean, and the temperature and weather in which it is to be kept. It soon became obvious that the skill of such men does not only lie in being able to buy the right meat at the right price at market. He had forged his reputation by his skill in selling it to the customer in exactly the right condition.

He said he liked mutton to hang for about nine days and that the proper time to kill it was in the autumn. Mutton is the flesh of a sheep a year or more old and, if it weren't hung, it would be as tough as old boots. It has now fallen out of fashion because most sheep are killed as lambs which would go bad, not ripen, if kept for more than a week anywhere but in a freezer. It is lean and mature meat which benefits from hanging – and game is not only lean but fully developed. The season to kill it is autumn, when flies have hibernated and the air is fresh and cool enough to allow it to hang and mature without going off.

So let the Common Market have all the immature, tasteless, fat meat they want to stuff in their freezers. Let them breathe garlic over each other to their hearts' content. But don't let them encourage our politicians to dream up laws to prevent those who enjoy the food of our forefathers from putting our feet under the table to a dish of old-fashioned gamey game.

6.   March Madness

Hares strip off their shyness in the spring. For most of the year they are as timid as the poets paint them but, when March blusters in, they lose their inhibitions.

My bedroom window sweeps almost down to the floor so that I can lie in bed and watch what goes on in the world outside. The edge of the wood is less than a hundred yards away and there is a turf paddock between it and the house.

For most of the year, a hare is a rare sight at such close quarters. They are either lying-up in thick woodland cover or crouching in their forms, or seats, in open fields around. At this time of year, the view from my bedroom is as good as from the front row in a dress circle. The lights go up as the sun shows through the trees to disclose a group of four or five hares grazing the short turf.

It is soon obvious that their minds are on other things than food. Pretending that this approach is accidental, a jack will graze gradually closer to an unsuspecting doe. Just as he thinks he has crept up on her unawares, he discovers she is not the fool he imagined. Before he knows where he is, she spins round and catches him a clout on his silk ear that sends him reeling yards away. He is understandably offended. In his book, doe hares are feminine and cooperative when spring is in the air. So he sidles back to sort her out.

They spar off at each other as sharp as kangaroos in a boxing ring, sending tussocks of silky hair floating on the wind. Women's Lib should work all right in a world of hares. The females are so much larger than the males that they are dominant anyway.

So, in no time at all, the jack gets a flea in his ear and he slinks quietly away to continue grazing, making out that the fracas had nothing to do with him. Not for long, though, for as soon as she has beaten off one suitor, the doe is accosted by another. Lying in bed, I watch them spar a bit and then run off in great chase-me-Charlie circles, as the doe tries to convince the world and herself that her honour is her all.

26

Nature built them for speed because they have so many enemies that ability to escape is vital for survival. Lots of dogs are faster than a hare but she usually escaped because she is more agile and can twist and turn more sharply. But in her courtship dance, she doubles and jinks for love of life instead of fear of death. When a dog is chasing her, she must win to save her skin. But when she is courting, she must lose to procreate her species.

When the breeding season starts, she has a litter about every four weeks until autumn, averaging almost four a litter. The number of young is maintained by a marvellous form of birth control. Not the sort of birth control that we use to limit the number born, but quite the opposite.

Foxes and stoats, weasels and hawks, owls and men with guns all prey on hares so it is vital that they reproduce as much as possible. So, if

A hare camouflaged on the plough.

a hare conceives a small litter of say two or three, she doesn't waste time allowing them to develop to normal birth. The embryos inside her are re-absorbed and she mates again on the chance that this time she will have a more economical size of litter.

This might be taking things to extremes, but leverets, or young hares, are immensely vulnerable. They do not spend the first part of their lives hidden safe below ground as rabbits do. They are born with their eyes open, fully furred and able to run away. Perhaps run is an exaggeration. They are so tiny and helpless that it is quite easy to pick them up in one's hand until they are several days old.

So their only way of escaping danger is to avoid being seen. The old does drop them on open ground or occasionally in a clump of nettles or grass. The tiny creatures lie perfectly still, relying only on their camouflage. To reduce the risk a little more, the doe separates the litter, leaving one on each of three or four forms.

The snag is that predators know by instinct that there is likely to be more than one leveret. If they find one accidentally, they search the surrounding area inch by inch. With odds like that against them, it is small wonder that hares have to operate their birth control in reverse.

7.   Persecuted Partridges

For once, something is better than expected. The humble partridge, which was a common bird in my youth, has declined in number over the years to a dangerous degree. So I am happy to announce that its population trend has recently taken a distinct turn for the better.

My first introduction to partridges was on a plate. My hostess presented me with half a beautifully rounded little bird, about the size of a small but plump pigeon. She had roasted it to a turn and served it with bread sauce, red currant jelly, braised celery and potatoes. It was delicious!

I followed up this introduction by making a date to join a party of sportsmen setting out to shoot partridge. So far as I remember, they shot about forty, which they were careful to calculate as twenty brace. Whether this piece of sporting jargon is in the interests of modesty, to make the slaughter sound less wholesale, or simply to bamboozle the uninitiated, I have yet to discover. But the fact remains that it was easy enough, in those days, to go out and shoot a score or so partridge on plenty of farms. One gentleman in East Anglia even ensured immortality amongst the famous (or infamous) by shooting a thousand in a day. Or possibly a thousand brace, I don't remember which.

Partridges became scarcer, not because sportsmen shot them to extinction but because farmers changed their methods of agriculture. Partridges are round, brown, plump little birds, with a lovely chestnut horseshoe on their breasts. They could give plenty of humans a start at being good parents and are devoted when rearing their chicks.

When the young grow up, they stay together as family parties, or coveys, until about February. Then they split up to pair with birds in the locality and each pair selects a breeding territory to make ready for the mating season. The snag is that they need insects and grain and they loved clover that was undersown to corn. They used to get all this by gleaning the stubbles that were left open to over-winter unploughed. Most stubbles are ploughed now as soon as the corn is harvested so that

29

prairies of bare soil have replaced the rich larder that kept partridges going over the hungry months.

Add to that catastrophe the fact that chemical pesticides now kill the insects needed by their chicks, and the hedges where they nest have been grubbed out, and it is obvious that they really are up against it.

But they are tougher than they seem. When I was a lad, growing up on the edge of the Black Country, houses were rapidly engulfing the farmland. There were still a few fields at the back of our house where there was always a pair or so of partridge, fighting a bitter rearguard action against the march of progress.

Town cats hunted them, vandals robbed their nests and men with guns shot them. Most lethal of all were poachers with nets. Partridges don't perch. They roost (or 'jug') on open ground, bunched up in tight circles, each bird facing outwards so that no enemy can creep up on them unawares.

Because of this, their droppings are also left in circles, about the size of dustbin lids so that any poacher walking over the field in daylight can mark the precise spot where a covey jugs. Then, on a dark night, he can return with a companion, dragging a net on two cords between them. If they have got their bearings right, one man passes to each side of the jugging covey. The net is drawn over them and dropped to prevent their escape the instant the poachers hear them flutter.

Gamekeepers thwarted this by strewing the field with small hawthorn branches which tangle the net, but a farmer friend of mine had an answer that was much more fun.

He took me with him – and we netted them ourselves! Instead of wringing their necks, as poachers would have done, we let them go again. It taught them a lesson that made them wary enough to keep clear of the cleverest poacher in future.

The partridge population has steadily declined since then, almost to danger level, but the last two summers seem to have given them a new lease of life. Their breeding results have been exceptionally good and many farmers have been so glad to see them around again that they have left odd corners to grow wild, for food and nesting cover, to encourage them.

So I am hoping that the winter will not be too hard on them and that they will have another kindly summer. Then, with a morsel of tolerance by sportsmen and help from friendly farmers, we may have plenty of jugging partridges in the fields once more.

8. The Modern Poacher's Status Symbol

The World Wildlife Fund's grant of £20,000 for conservation in Britain is to be spent on a vigilante force to guard animals and birds and plants which cannot be protected by 'normal' methods. Rare orchids are being ravished by wild orchid hunters. The sons (or daughters) of old-fashioned poachers are more sophisticated than their dads.

They are now too educated to knock-off the squire's rabbits for Sunday dinner. They and their friends are in a smarter set where status symbols consist of rare wild flowers to decorate their cocktail cabinets. These modern sneak thieves have exchanged their purse nets and ferrets for a garden trowel. Their raids are carried out with such expertise that rare military and monkey orchids in Berkshire and Buckinghamshire are growing rarer, in spite of electrified fences and other wiles dreamed up by local naturalists.

This selfish fringe of educated thieves are prepared to plunder the rarest species for the kick of having a more exotic flower arrangement than their neighbours.

Botanists who have been making detailed records of species in need of protection, dare not plot the precise location of their finds. If they do, there is nothing to find next time they call.

It is now an offence to pick, let alone uproot, many of our wild flowers, but modern protection laws have little deterrent effect. Fines have not caught up with inflation and too many woolly magistrates see nothing wrong in picking a few wild flowers.

Wild birds are in almost as much danger. The Protection of Birds Act made it illegal to take the eggs or disturb the nests of many British birds which are not active pests to agriculture. Yet there are still louts at large prepared to plunder them for profit – or for kicks.

The Royal Society for the Protection of Birds erected a hide within a safe distance of the nest of a rare osprey. It gave pleasure to thousands without inconveniencing the birds. Even so, it proved necessary to

A falconer with two hooded hawks.

surround the tree with electronic warning devices and barbed wire, in spite of which the vandals nearly cut it down.

Birds of prey seem to be at more risk than most. When I was a boy, you could almost count the practising falconers on the fingers of one hand. It is a spectacular but specialist sport so that the number of people with both the expertise and time to train and fly a hawk is very limited.

It has now degenerated into the glamour class. Exhibitions of falcons flying to the lure are a great attraction at the Game Fair, and a film about a lad who had a trained kestrel put dangerous ideas into many boys' heads. One year, the British Falconers Club managed to persuade the organisers of the Game Fair not to have a falconry display, largely because it so inflates the demand for hawks and encourages unauthorised robbing of their nests.

But the damage is done. The demand is such that wretched birds can now be seen tethered by the leg to blocks in suburban gardens and even in city flats. However well meaning they are, most of the would-be falconers have neither the time nor the knowledge to cope with them, so that these wildest of birds are doomed to fret away their lives in miserable captivity.

Before firearms were invented, hawking was a serious method of filling the larder as well as being a specialised sport. The birds were housed in 'mews' and the number of mews flats in every old town or city is some indication of how popular they were. Every nobleman kept his own professional falconer whose full-time job it was to minister to his hawks.

In spite of such popularity, demand was ruthlessly, but simply, controlled so that it did not outstrip supply. Only a king or emperor could have an eagle and a nobleman a gyr falcon. So it went on, down the scale, to the parson who was the lowest form of life in hawking terms! He had to make do with a humble sparrow-hawk.

In our age of equality, no such sensible rules apply.* Any unsuitable person can get a hawk if he gets a permit, and permits are not difficult to come by. The proof of that pudding is in the eating. Demand for birds of prey has rocketed astronomically so that an eagle will fetch four figures, and a peregrine several hundred pounds.

See No. 31.

The RSPB will be spending almost £3000 this year to protect golden eagles and peregrine falcones. A few years ago, peregrines were almost wiped out by chemicals used on farms. The human pests who harry them now are a greater peril than any poisonous pesticide.

9. Beauty Can Do Without The Beast

I have never understood why so many beautiful women are dissatisfied with the attractions that Nature gave them. Girls, who are an eyeful by any sandards, still hanker after additional sex-status symbols. They yearn to camouflage their charms beneath the skins of rare animals they cannot even eat.

Recently, the Endangered Species (Import and Export) Act 1976 was passed and it has just become law. This is bureaucratic jargon for the fait that it is now illegal to import or export the skins of some species that are growing so rare that their survival is in peril.

In the past few years, forests all over the world have been destroyed and swamps cleared for timber or to get extra agricultural land. Tigers and leopards and cheetahs have been concentrated into shrinking refuges until they are too overcrowded to thrive. Their increasing rarity has inflated their price which women regard as a yardstick of their own desirability.

As long ago as 1973, there was a convention in Washington to try to control 'International Trade in Endangered Species of Wild Flora and Fauna'. The object was to try to stop the slaughter of a whole range of species whose survival is threatened because they are being persecuted to the point of extinction.

Despite the pompous title, the convention came up with practical rules to safeguard species ranging from tigers and elephants to cheetahs and a few rare birds. There was predictable opposition by vested interests and it took a couple of years for the United Kingdom to meet the requirements of the convention.

After a year in step, we have now passed the Endangered Species Act which has given our promises legal backing. Far more important, the Act provides for changes to be made in the list of species affected by making an Order covering various species.

36

It is now illegal for the vainest woman to buy the skins of black or white Colobus monkeys with which to embellish their charms. They are no longer allowed to trade in turtle meat or the eggs of birds other than poultry.

Much as I sympathise with such threatened foreign species, I am old-fashioned enough to believe that charity begins at home. So I was particularly delighted to discover that it is now illegal to trade in the skins of otters. Although British law has given protection to some wild birds and plants for some years, we have been terribly slow to do anything about animals.

The first British animal to receive protection was the badger. That was not until the 1973 Badger Act. It was hardly worth the paper on which it was written because it only made it illegal to kill or take a badger except by 'authorised persons'. As an 'authorised person' included the occupier of the land, anyone authorised in writing by him, anyone authorised by the local authority or various ministries, the protection was illusory.

I have studied badgers for over twenty years, and make no secret of the fact that I have great affection and admiration for them. They are so tough that a few pest officers, working office hours, are unlikely to wipe them out.

Otters are quite a different matter. They are in far greater peril and it would have been more logical to pass a law to protect them before any other British animal. Their way of life limits their choice of where they can live mainly to the banks of rivers and lakes. They have been persecuted for centuries by gamekeepers and water bailiffs and otter hunters so that the need for self-preservation has made them extremely shy.*

Disturbance by boaters, fishermen and hikers has driven them from otherwise suitable stretches of water. River boards in drainage operations have destroyed the trees and roots where they breed. Farm effluent and poisonous pesticides poison frogs and fish – and anything that eats the victims.

If any animal needs protection, it is the British otter.† So I welcome the legislation which makes it illegal to buy or sell their skins – but it is still only scratching at the surface.

* *See* No. 18.
† *See* No. 22.

10. Something To Honk About

The arrival of spring was heralded by a trumpeting dawn chorus that almost bounced me out of bed. Whatever misery the weatherman forecast, our Canada geese left us in no doubt that things are better than they seem.

Watch a flock grazing the short turf by the water's edge and you will notice that one stands erect as a guardsman on sentry-go, while the others feed in peace. After a while, he will start to feed while one of the others takes over the job of lookout man. If a shooter pokes his head over the skyline or a fox sneaks along the hedgerow towards the feeding flock, a honk of alarm brings them all to attention. They take wing and fly to safety while danger is still too far away to matter.

Things are different while the goose is sitting. However vigilant the gander may be, it is always possible for a fox to stalk up under the cover of darkness and bite off the sitting bird's head.

So our geese wisely choose the island in the pool. To get near them, a fox would have to swim and risk an extremely uncomfortable ducking if the gander spotted him half way across.

When the goslings hatch, they come across to feed on the sweet turf of the paddock by day but return to their island haven before dusk falls. It always surprises me to hear what a fuss they make when they return. Their voice is a loud, trumpeting honk so that when they fly over at night, it is easy to understand the country belief that a ghostly pack of hounds is hunting lost souls in the sky. If colliers heard them on their way to the pit, they took it as a bad omen and returned home in case they had an accident at work!

So there is never any doubt about when our birds come back, although most birds are secretive and shy about letting anyone know their detailed plans for nesting.

I say 'ours' although it is they who have adopted us rather than we

38

who own them. Although we see nothing of them through the winter, they arrive with spring to nest as surely as the swallows do.

This was not always so because when we bought Goat Lodge sixteen years ago, there wasn't a goose on the pool. There is a marvellous bush telegraph among wild creatures. Although different species may not speak the same language, they are quick to get the message when times improve. Word soon got around that our wood had been converted into a quiet and secluded residence. A taste of security is as attractive to animals and birds as it is to us – when we are lucky enough to find it. Timid deer grew bolder and shy herons thrived. Wild duck nested in the shrubbery right by the house – but no geese came.

Eventually, I grew fed up and hand-reared a clutch of goslings, leaving them free to join their wild relatives when winter came. Since then we have never been without them. They arrive to prospect in

Canada geese have an aggressive courtship.

March and have chosen a nest site and laid a clutch of eggs in April.

This year, they treated us to a positive festival of sound. Instead of the usual duet, telling each other how delighted they were to be back, no less than fourteen came. Obviously this unusual number of Canada geese had decided to give our pool star rating which accounted for the row they made. It wasn't so much an anthem of thanksgiving as a hymn of hate – because they all wanted the same site.

They honked and hooted till our sleep became impossible. One great old gander retreated to the far end of the pool, not because he was frightened but to add impetus to his charge. Then, flapping over the surface, he gathered momentum until he was an irresistible force approaching his rival, the immovable object. They thumped and buffeted each other until one conceded defeat and retreated to find an alternative nesting site.

Instead of one pair living in elegant ease on the island in our pool, we have three pairs. They do not exactly have to live in squalor but it is almost cheek-by-jowl. There is one pair on the island, as usual, one in the reed bed at the far end of the pool and one in some reeds at the near corner. Those on the island have the best pitch for they are safe from foxes. But nature never did believe in mollycoddling weaklings. Surplus populations are provided as a crop to feed the predators.

11. Pulling The Wool Over A Foster Mother's Eyes

As maternity homes go, the sheep-yard past our wood is superb. Capacity for 800 expectant patients, skilled obstetricians in times of crisis, and private wards for mums with new-born babies. Sheep may pay for no National Health stamps, but the standard of attention they receive merits five-star rating by anybody's standards.

When I was a lad, a competent shepherd was expected to manage 150 or 200 sheep in the field or on the hill. Climbing up and down the mountainside, trying to be in the right place at the right time, was a frustrating business. If he turned his back for an instant, a carrion crow could fly down to blind a lamb in the process of birth, or a fox could steal it before the ewe was strong enough to get on her feet to defend it.

A shower of wintry rain could chill a lamb beyond the strength or willpower to survive, and ewes which rolled on to their backs (or were 'cast') often died if not assisted in righting themselves. Under such conditions an average of a lamb-and-a-half per ewe was pretty good but things have changed since then.

The modern fashion is to 'yard' the flock in winter. Large covered yards are bedded in soft straw and divided into compartments which will house twenty-five or fifty ewes. This is so that they don't crowd each other at the feeding troughs and injure their unborn young.

The shepherd knows when they are due to lamb because the rams are fitted with harness containing coloured pads which stain the ewes when they are mated. The colour of the pads is changed at intervals. So he divides them into batches due to lamb at about the same time.

They spend the winter dry and warm, fed on hay or silage and corn so that, by spring, they are in superb condition to lamb. As the coloured patch on their backs denotes that their time is drawing near, they are shifted up into lambing pens under skilled supervision. On a nearby farm, 800 ewes are yarded together and programmed to lamb at convenient intervals over about a month.

41

Scientific breeding has raised the average number of lambs so that many ewes have twins and some triplets. They do not make enough milk to cope with triplets very well, so one lamb is taken from most ewes that have triplets, and fostered on to a ewe that has lost a lamb or has only one.

This was an awful business in the old days because sheep are reluctant to accept strange lambs that do not smell of them. The traditional method was to foster only on the ewes that had lost a lamb. The dead lamb was skinned and the skin stitched round the stranger that the shepherd wanted fostered. When the ewe turned to smell the lamb, it smelled of her, and she would usually be persuaded to accept it. But it was a chancy and messy business.

Now, when each ewe has her lambs, she is put in a single 'side ward' made of hurdles or straw bales so that she can spend a day or so with her lamb undisturbed. Each gets to know the smell and voice of the other so that, when they are turned out with the flock to graze, each lamb knows the sound of its mother's voice and each ewe knows the smell of her own lamb.

When the shepherd wants to foster a spare lamb on to a strange ewe, he puts the ewe and lamb into an individual pen but he fastens the ewe's head through a slot from which she cannot withdraw it. She stands there, as if her head were in a pillory and, when the strange lamb gets hungry, he goes and helps himself to milk at his private milk bar. With her head held fast, there is nothing the foster mother can do to stop him and, within twenty-four hours, her milk has passed through him.

From then on he acquires her smell so that it is possible to release her head because, once he has her taint, she cannot tell the difference between him and her own lamb, and she will accept him as her own flesh and blood.

A few orphans still have to be reared as 'cades' on the bottle, and that is where many a shepherd's wife or children come into their own. Most nice children love helping on the farm at lambing time by being nursemaid to the cade lambs.

12.   This Dodo Isn't Dead

Dodo arrived in this country in 1936 and ended up on a counter of the Wolverhampton Woolworths. The only remarkable fact about that is he is almost certainly the only survivor from the large consignment of tortoises captured in Morocco that year and shipped to this country as pets. Forty-one years later, he is still going strong!

His luck came when he caught the eye of Mrs Johnson who took him home as a pet for her grandson, Derek. The Johnson family have lavished unstinting care on him ever since. Young Derek, who has been

Dodo the tortoise.

a friend of mine for many years and illustrates my books, was not then old enough to take full responsibility.

So his father put a low wire netting fence round the garden to prevent Dodo from straying into danger. He also built him a 'bungalow', three bricks high, roofed with a paving slab and furnished with soft hay.

Dodo took to this at once and every summer evening, for the last forty-one years, he returns to his bungalow and tucks himself up for the night. If the weather is fine, he will walk round the garden for four or five hours during the day, helping himself to the most succulent lettuce or browsing on clover or dandelion in the lawn, or any choice flowers that take his fancy.

But he is not satisfied with fending for himself. If any of the Johnson family invade his territory in the garden, he shambles up (if he will pardon the phrase) to be hand-fed with thin slices of cucumber or thinly sliced apple. If he finds a juicy strawberry growing in the garden, he is quite capable of wolfing it down before anyone can get round to picking it.

Lots of people have bought tortoises like Dodo as pets for the kids, and nearly all of them die during the first year. They are imported from their warm Mediterranean shores, dumped in the garden and left to fend for themselves. Their conditions of transport are dreadful, and they usually grow so thin that they practically rattle about in their shells. It is so often a cruel business that I should like to see their import stopped.

Dodo is the exception because of the care that has been lavished upon him. The critical period of his life occurs in mid-October each year. As the nights draw in and grow colder, he begins to get drowsy but, in spite of the urge to fall asleep, his instinct drives him to wander restlessly round the garden, looking for somewhere to dig himself in for his winter hibernation. Given the opportunity, his favourite place would be the compost heap, and he has disappeared under the rotting vegetation several times. To leave him there would sign his death sentence. As compost heaps mature, their temperature rises and gases are given off during decomposition. If he didn't suffocate, he would wake up and emerge into cold winter air which would kill him.

So when autumn comes, Dodo is collected every night and put into a comfortable box of hay under the stairs where it is easy to inspect him frequently during the winter months. For a week or so, he wakes during the day and is put out into the garden to feed a little and wander round, but as temperatures fall, he gradually gets more drowsy until he goes into the deep sleep of hibernation.

He stays under the stairs, where it is cool but never frosty, until the end of March when he wakes up to meet the spring. Derek Johnson then cleans him up and puts him out for a few hours in the garden during the warmer parts of the day. As the sunshine warms his blood, it courses through his veins, but he never gets the urge to do anything more exciting than steal the family strawberries.

A few years ago, a mate was bought for him but the romance never blossomed. Finally, she died.

The original Mrs Johnson, who first invested in Dodo, has long since died; so has her son, Derek's father. Derek himself is beginning to feel the effects of old age so the care of Dodo has fallen on young Ian, the fourth generation of the Johnson family to be given the responsibility. He is the great-grandson of the original purchaser.

So many generations dedicated to the care of one pet from Woolworths is a rare example of human devotion.

13. · Cold Feet For Dinner

Our heavy clay soil squelches in protest at every footfall, endorsing the fact that February Filldyke is no old wives' tale. I have knotted the muscles in my back, shoving drain rods through congested culverts in the wood, and dug out ditches, silted up with leaves from last year's drought.

My dreams have been uneasy visions of havoc downstream if the weight of water causes the banks of our pool to collapse. So I clear the sluice every morning. The hotache in my fingers is a small price to pay for knowing that the overflow is working well.

Continuous rain at our last house caused us even worse problems. Instead of sympathising with the hazards of neighbours downstream, we had plenty of immediate worries of our own. We had a lovely pool, just across the drive, fed by a clear mill stream that rose in the hills of Cannock Chase. We kept exotic ducks, which decorated the lawn – and ate some of the choicest plants in the garden. We fell asleep to the soothing sound of a waterfall and – in summer – it was idyllic.

But in weather like we have had for the last few weeks, there was a serious risk that the pool outlet would be inadequate to cope with winter floods. Several times, while we lived there, the pool level rose until it flooded the lawn and lapped along the edges of the drive. The front door was twenty feet away – and the front door step was very shallow! Another six inches higher and the water level would have set the downstairs carpet awash.

Even in hilly country, it is deceptively easy to pick the wrong site. A friend of ours bought an isolated stone cottage in Wales for a holiday home. He and his family spent their leisure hours smartening it up and installing modern conveniences and a septic tank in the garden. They were so proud of it when they had finished that they threw a magnificent house-warming party for their friends.

House-warming turned out to be an ill-chosen term! They had just settled down to a superb meal, cooked by the hostess and served by romantic candlelight, when the host noticed the guest on his right shuffling in her seat. He was speculating what could have given his well-mannered neighbour such a fit of the fidgets when he noticed that his own feet were uncomfortably cold.

A storm, higher up in the hills, had overflowed the mountain stream and a torrent of water was sieving through the dry stone wall, and had turned the dining-room into a lake. Luckily, the other wall was just as porous so that the surplus water trickled through the wall on the lower side of the house to flow on down the valley.

The water supply to the cottage was still as primitive as the drainage had been. A spring, higher up the hill, had been piped to a stone trough from which every drop of water had to be carried in a bucket! The snag was that the trough was on the opposite side of the road and my friend feared that the officials in the local planning office might be a little stuffy.

So he decided not to mention it. He and his son waited until the last revellers had staggered home from the local inn, and then set to work like navvies through the night. When the sun rose over the hill, they had dug a trench across the road – and filled it in again. At the bottom of the trench ran their pipe which has delivered pure spring water ever since. Free of charge. A slight scar on a remote Welsh road is all that remains to prove that a respectable doctor and his son can move a mountain if they have the right incentive.

The mystery of water has always fascinated me, so my admiration for an ancestor of the Duke of Devonshire knows no bounds. On a visit to Russia, he had been shown a fountain which was the apple of the Czar's eye. It spurted its jet 180 ft. above ground. When he came home, the Duke decided to wipe the Czar's eye and have a fountain that was even bigger and better, at Chatsworth, his seat in Derbyshire.

He called in a gang of men to harness the streams and river on the moors above the house. They dug drains and ditches and culverts to a reservoir, and piped the water down to a lake in front of the house. The overflow cascaded down a series of waterfalls half-a-mile long and now the fountain in the centre of the lake throws up a jet like that from a firehose, 200 ft. high.

14. The Battle In The Woods

For the first time since we came here, the rides in our wood are quite presentable. I shall never forget the first time I saw the place. The cottage had been empty and deserted for more than two years, and there was a jungle of nettles between the house and the outside privy that made haste an impossibility.

The timber at the far side of the wood had been felled and the woodmen were in the process of dragging out the tree trunks. The machine they used for the process, 'timber-drug' they called it, was a rumbling giant with steel tracks that might have come off an outsize tank. It was chained to a four-wheeled carriage, strutted with a steel pole spanning the two pairs of wheels, and the trunks of oak and beech, stripped naked of their branches, were lashed to the carriage with wire hawsers.

I imagine that the first few journeys out of the wood had only cut the rides into relatively minor ruts. By the time I arrived, the traffic had been so heavy and continuous that the great wheels squelched th ough sticky mire to their axles. I hate to see proud trees humbled and toppled in the mud. The sight of the mutilated woodland floor somehow made their plight seem worse.

After we took possession, I spent the next ten years or so trying to heal over the havoc. The first priority was to be able to get round the place at all. The rides where the woodmen had dragged their timber soon looked all right. Lush grass grew knee-high and camouflaged the fact that they were rutted, pot-holed and cratered as deep as a battlefield. They may have been fine for tanks and bulldozers, but to walk on them was like stepping in a man trap.

So the first job was to cut the grass and expose the pitfalls that lay beneath, and that was easier said than done. I had got a motor scythe like the machines they use to cut the grass verges and the inaccessible spots on golf courses. In the advertisements, they always depict shapely wenches in briefs and bras and summer shoes, leaning nonchalantly on the handles of scythes like mine as they turn hayfields into tennis lawns.

48

The rides at Goat Lodge: before (author with the lurchers) ...

and after (author with Tick) the battle.

I should like to have seen the girl in the ad. take her scythe along our woodland ries!

I am fairly tough but, after an hour of mowing, I felt that I should have had an easier passage in a match with a champion all-in wrestler.

Eventually I barbered the surface vegetation short enough to see what lay beneath – and the devil I could then see seemed worse than his invisible predecessor. The smooth green paths turned out to be hideous ploughed fields, but the sight of their stark reality drove home the truth that there was no reason why I couldn't deal with them as if they were normal farmland.

So I got out my ancient tractor and hitched on my neighbour's disc harrows. I cultivated those rides as a farmer would till a field and, when I had tamed the knobs and hollows, I worked it smooth. Then I dragged chain harrows over it, to give the surface a fine tilth and seeded it with grass.

It took several years for my labours to blossom. For one thing, there was no hard bottom to the rides so that, whenever the weather was wet, the wheels of my tractor made ruts like railway lines.

So Tom, our local blacksmith, made me a roller. And when Tom makes a tool, it puts the tiny contraptions of agricultural merchants in the shade. It doesn't have the final coat of paint that makes conventional farm machinery look as pretty as the replicas that have replaced the toy soldiers for modern kids, but it works.

My roller started life as a huge iron pipe, 2 ft 6 ins. across, with metal an inch in thickness. Tom welded two round plates, to make each end solid, and fitted a yoke so that I could hitch it to my tractor. Stripped naked, as it was, it weighed the best part of a ton.

To make perfection better, he fitted a screw plug so that when I really wanted some 'graunch', as he put it, I could fill it with water and double the weight. It pounded my rides down to super-highways and, when they were grown with grass and mown, they were a sight to be proud of.

15. This Mimic Could Give Mike Yarwood The Bird

Dawn was just breaking when a curlew started calling in our yard. At least, it sounded like a curlew. It was that glorious lilting, bubbling song I always associate with wild places.

When we came to Goat Lodge, years ago, the farm at the other side of the wood was still untamed parkland. It was spattered with stag-headed oak trees and rippling streams bubbling through acres of rushes and marsh. The land is more than 500 feet above sea level and, until it was drained, it was perfect curlew country.

Curlews are large wading birds, with streaky brown plumage and long, strongly curved bills. They love the grass moors and bogs of hilly country and they make the solitary places echo with their wild haunting song.

They deserted the parkland near our wood when it was drained and ploughed, so I went out to investigate what one could be doing in our yard. I couldn't locate it at first. The song was plain enough, but it sounded faint and far away. It also came from only one direction while curlew so often sing in flight that their music seems stereophonic.

As so often happens when I am tempted out of bed too soon, the answer proved to be an anti-climax. The maestro wasn't a curlew at all. It was a starling mimicking one. I could have chucked a brick at him for sending me up, but his artistry stayed my hand. His virtuosity was such that he made Mike Yarwood seem an amateur! Halfway through his curlew routine, he switched to the yaffling cry of a green woodpecker and, if I hadn't seen him, I should have been foxed again.

We do have green woodpeckers in the wood and often hear them raise the echoes with demonic laughter that might easily be mistaken for a sinister spook. The song of our starling was a dead ringer until, out of the blue, he put on his curlew hat again and sang his heavenly refrain.

I can never understand why so many folk dislike starlings. They say they are 'common' and dirty and greedy, but some of the nicest people I know are all of those things but still have irresistible charm. Look at the iridescent plumage of a starling glinting in the sun and you must agree it is more beautiful than most of the rarities that birdlovers rave about.

Shut your eyes and listen to his song. It is not the extrovert yelling of a blackbird, pouring out hymns of hate at all possible rivals. The starling sings quietly, more to amuse himself than to challenge rivals or to secure a place in the avian pop ratings. It is a quiet soliloquy, recalling for his own delight the highlights of far-off places and melodies he'd heard there.

I wondered where our starling had spent the winter and only had to listen to make a pretty shrewd guess. I could see, in my mind's eye, the hills of central Wales, with hanging woods of oak and birch softening the outlines where uplands merged with the valley below. I have spent so many happy holidays in wild country around the Brecon hills that it only took a snatch of the music in our yard to scoop pictures that had lain forgotten in the back of my mind for years.

When the woodpecker yaffled, I suddenly saw a pair of buzzards soaring graceful and silent as gliders in the sky.

16. Malpractice In The Marketplace

Last week, my job took me into a cattle market for a whole day. It is a long time since I was in a market and, at first, it rekindled many childhood memories. In my young days, cattle trucks were luxuries, used only by rich farmers and, if it was necessary to send beasts very far, they went by rail.

Being born at Bloxwich, our nearest auctions were at Lichfield and Wolverhampton and I often spent a day of my school holidays helping a friend drive a bunch of cattle to one or other market. It doesn't sound much of a job but what always happened was that the cattle started off at full gallop, diving into the gardens of anyone foolish enough to have left the gate open. So the first half hour was usually spent retrieving them and, if the owner also happened to have got up at around six o'clock, it was a question of talking one's way out of trouble.

It is surprising how niggly people can get over a small matter of half a dozen bullocks on their lawn! We found that the best way to deal with such situations was to pretend to be absolutely stone deaf and, if our antagonists could shout loud enough to enlist the help of unfriendly neighbours, we pretended to be half-witted as well!

After a bit, the cattle, unused to such strenuous exercise, lost their enthusiasm for exploration and escape and our main job was to coax and bully them along.

For a lad, it was all marvellous fun and I never got around to wondering what the cattle thought about being driven further than they liked to a strange place, which was usually nothing more than a temporary lodging on the way to the condemned cell. We had always had about enough when we arrived so we repaired to the local as soon as they were safely lodged in the sales pens.

My friend always bought me a cider which was more than I was allowed at home, and we returned to the sale yard in time for the excitement of seeing the beasts we had driven so far put under the auctioneer's hammer. The feelings of the victims were the last thing to cross our minds.

Last week brought back all those memories after forty years or so. This time, it wasn't cattle they were selling, but sheep. Lambs straight off the Welsh hills and the first thing that caught my eye was the look in theirs.

I never thought of sheep showing any expression at all. So much wool camouflages whatever crosses their minds, as effectively as it would ours if we swathed our faces in Balaclava helmets. But their movements gave the game away. They were rigid with apprehension. Only the fact that their instinct had taught them that there is safety in numbers prevented those agile mountain sheep taking a high jump over the hurdles of the pens and legging it back to the solitude of their beloved hills.

Market day.

I suppose there were a thousand or so to go under the hammer and almost all of them were lambs destined for the butcher. They had had a short life, and I wondered if it had been a happy one.

Certainly the latter part was not. As each pen was sold, a man climbed in and, using a pair of pliers, he punched a hole in each lamb's ear large enough to put your finger through. Just like that, with no ceremony – and no anaesthetic. The enormity of it hit me like a pole axe. It seemed such an unnecessary and brutal thing to do.

And why, do you think, it should be so vital to inflict such callous disfiguration? It is to stop greedy owners from fiddling a little extra subsidy. A bonus is paid, once only, on some animals sold and the wide boys discovered that they could take beasts to market, buy them in, and so get the Government subsidy more than once. Or that is what they told me in the market. No subsidy would be paid on any sheep that had a hole in its ear because the hole would be proof that it had been paid already.

The men who were perpetrating this horror were neither deliberately cruel nor sadistic: they were simply following their instructions. It is yet another case of the right hand not knowing what the left hand is doing. We pass laws for humane slaughter, saying that no cow or sheep or pig may be killed unless it has first been stunned by a humane killer or other device.

Yet followers of some religions are allowed to observe the ritual slaughter that would not be tolerated by Christians. And our animals are sent abroad alive, under dreadful conditions, to be killed by archaic methods rather than offend a few foreign customers, or export their frozen carcases.

It is high time we put our house in order.

17.   Road Hogs

A recent headline will take quite a bit of beating for inaccuracy. 'Sheep Initiates Milk Race Crash', it said. The text described how some compulsive two-wheeled athlete was scorching up the miles with his nose a few inches above his front tyres. Not having eyes in the top of his head, he doubtless found it difficult to see where he was going and fetched up in a heap on the tarmac when he collided with a sheep.

The inaccuracy in the headline stems from the implication that it was the sheep which 'initiated' the crash. The frustrated racer may have resented the fact that what he regarded as no more than a hunk of animated mutton had put him out of the prize money.

But I bet the gently grazing sheep still thinks that the cause of the accident had nothing to do with him but rested solely with the silent human projectile that didn't know that sheep often cross mountain roads. I trust that no permanent damage was done to the incomparable Welsh lamb and that his adversary has now finished rubbing his head – or whichever end he landed on.

The incident illustrates the damage that befalls both wildlife and domestic stock through road accidents, most of which could be prevented by reasonable care. My job takes me over about 20,000 miles of English roads every year and I am often sickened by the havoc I see.

Unlike sheep and cyclists, motorists pay specific tax to use the roads in addition to the general taxes extorted from us all. Some of them think that this gives them absolute priority. This lunatic fringe resent or disregard everything that gets in their way and only agility on the part of their victim separates the quick from the dead!

Since my daily journeys sometimes involve a couple of hundred miles to a job, and the same back, I am often out before dawn and after dusk. By keeping my eyes open, I see nocturnal animals going home and deer and rabbits and hares coming out to feed before more sensible men are awake. The verges of country roads at dawn attract a wide variety of birds which gather there for 'gritting'. Birds' digestions are so designed that they need hard grit in their gizzards to grind up the corn they feed on. So, for an hour or so after dawn, I often see partridges and pheasants and wood pigeons foraging within a few feet of the highway.

One summer, a motorist in front of me deliberately swerved to hit a hen pheasant. It was a despicable method of poaching, but I suppose he was too ignorant or unskilful to poach by traditional methods and too mean to pay for legitimate sport. Far worse, the brood of chicks that the pheasant was sure to have recently hatched were doomed to die a sudden death by predators or at a slower rate from cold and hunger.

All of which I told the intrepid driver when he stopped to gather his spoil, in words, I trust, plain enough to penetrate his limited intelligence. I left him to find out for himself that the bruised and battered remains would probably putrefy, at that time of year, so that it would be dangerous to eat them.

In areas like Cannock Chase, sixty or seventy deer are killed on the roads each year, and in the New Forest and on Exmoor ponies suffer in spite of notices clearly warning of their presence.

It is reasonable to spend money to keep wild creatures off motorways and to impose heavy fines on the owners of domestic stock which stray there. They were designed and built, at great expense, to prevent increasing traffic snarling to a standstill. But it is quite impracticable to restrict the movement of sheep and cattle on the sparse grazing of remote hill pastures or to teach deer, hedgehogs and birds that they trespass if they cross a road.

One of the few advantages I can see from our runaway inflation is that many local authorities have economised on verge spraying. Too many of them have an urban 'tidy' mind about the grass along the roadsides. It has to be as weed-free as a city park.

This year, country lanes and roads have been lined with the delicate white froth of Queen Anne's Lace, bluebells and stitchwort. Not only have they been more beautiful than usual, but the extra foliage has narrowed the lanes a bit. Because there looks that bit less room, the traffic goes just a little bit slower. Slow enough, I hope, for motorists to take evasive action if a chicken crosses a road, or for cyclists to wobble round a sheep.

18.   Stop Hounding The Otter!

Pressure is mounting again for the preservation of the otter. I hope this time it succeeds.* I have had personal experience with most field sports. 'Blood sports' is the favoured phrase of those who would have them stopped because the idea of spilling blood is more emotive.

I believe there are three major factors to consider when the subjects of hunting and shooting are being discussed. One is the degree of cruelty involved. The second is the effect on the species being hunted. And the third is whether it is ethical to enjoy that sort of sport anyhow. So far as I am concerned I regard it as no business of mine whether other people enjoy it or not. It is their private affair and I feel in no way qualified to preach to them.

Cruelty, I think, is relative and whether it is preferable to die by hounds or gunshots or for a predator, like the fox, to die slowly from disease, is a subjective decision. Isn't it odd that fishermen seem above criticism? I would not like a hook through my lip until I drowned, would you?

In any case, more animals suffer for longer in markets and slaughterhouses every week than at the hands of the field sportsman. I would certainly do all in my power to alleviate that first and to encourage authorities to ban the sale of live animals to foreign countries where they do not enforce civilised methods of slaughter.

So far as otter hunting goes, whoever wishes to ban it has my vote. I was a member of the Staffordshire Otterhounds when I was in my teens and I went out with them whenever I could. The procedure was to meet on a river and to set off, either up or down stream, with some of the hounds on each bank.

Otters are tremendous wanderers and they often travel miles to feed on the fish they catch before returning, at dawn, to their same lair, or holt, under the roots of a tree by the bank. Hounds would scent where they had been and follow the trail, or 'drag', to where they had holed-up in what they hoped would be a safe retreat. A terrier would then be sent down the hole, like a ferret after a rat, and flush out the quarry into the water.

See No. 19.

Otters are superb swimmers and, while they are fresh, have no difficulty in diving under hounds and swimming for the safety of another holt. The snag was that it wasn't safe. Hounds would soon mark, from their scent, where they had hidden and the terrier would flush them out again.

The hunt followers lined the bank and watched for what they called the otter's 'chain'. This was the chain of bubbles which he had exhaled as he swam underwater, and they gave away his position as surely as if he had stuck a periscope out of the water. Even as an unimaginative youth, I regarded this as most unsporting help for hounds and I never divulged the otter's secret when I spotted from his chain where he had hidden.

You might think, from my description, that every otter the hounds hunted was doomed. Not so. I went out scores of times and never saw

The now disbanded Hawkstone Otter Hounds being entered into a very low River Teify at Cellan, Dyfed.

an otter killed. Then, why, you might ask, am I steamed up about stopping otter hunting?

Not because of the cruelty. I doubt if it is worse than ratting which I enjoyed for many years without anyone ever following me with banners saying 'Ban ratting'. I would ban otter hunting because circumstances have caused such a decline in the otter population since I was young that they are now as much an endangered species as rare hawks or barn owls or kingfishers.

They have been hounded out of existence not by hunting so much as by human disturbance. River authorities, in their frenzy to turn rivers into drains which waste water instead of conserving it, have grubbed out scores of ancient otter holts with bulldozers. The only otters you are now likely to see are in the wilds of Scotland, Wales or Ireland or the decreasing solitudes of England.

So I would ban otter hunting, not because it kills many otters but because it adds to the already intolerable degree of their disturbance. By the same token, I would ban shooters and walkers and fishermen from stretches of river to give seclusion for their holts. Otherwise, otters will soon join those beautiful animals and birds we have allowed to be persecuted to the point of extinction.

19. The Year Of The Ladybird

I shall always look back on 1976 as the Year of the Ladybird. The longest-toothed weatherman cannot remember a drought like it and, by mid-summer, there was a plague of aphids which threatened us with famine. There were blackflies on the beans, greenfly on the roses and honeysuckle and tomatoes, while almost every other garden crop seemed to be shuffling off to extinction.

Gardeners and farmers reached for their spray guns charged with deadly pesticides. But agricultural chemists are not as clever as they think against disaster of such proportions. It is easy enough to spray a cherished rosebud or even a field of corn or sugar beet. But that only kills the pests in a very limited zone.

The aphids which thrived last summer swarmed on every bush and tree and hedgeside and piece of waste ground. It was quite impossible to spray them all so that there were always survivors to reinfest 'clean' patches.

It was the drought which had provided the ideal conditions for the aphids to thrive in. A normal English summer does not go many days without a shower. And a raindrop landing on anything as small and fragile as a greenfly or a blackfly hits it like a waterfall. It dislodges it from its stronghold on the plant and swills it out of harm's way. Drought conditions not only produced temperatures which encouraged insects to breed prolifically but the absence of rain left the progeny to breed unhindered.

We passed through the shadow of a serious famine which was only averted by the arrival of swarms of ladybirds. I have always regarded ladybirds with the greatest affection. As a kid, I never came across one without perching him/her on the end of my finger and reciting the rhyme:

'Ladybird, ladybird, fly away home,
Your house is on fire, your children are gone.'

At this stage, the tiny beetle, incensed by my waggling finger, would open his horny wing cases and fly away, though I never discovered whether he flew home.

We used to have great competitions to see who could find ladybirds with the greatest variety of spots on them, or who could collect specimens of different colours or with most spots.

The significance of the bad luck foretold in the rhyme only dawned on me after the drought we had this year. By the time there really was a plague of aphids, which nobody could do much about by conventional means, the ladybirds arrived.

Ladybirds lay eggs which hatch into insignificant larvae which look, at first glance, like little grey slugs equipped with the six legs of a conventional insect. They look puny and harmless, but viewed through a powerful magnifying glass, they take on sinister proportions. Through the eyes of a greenfly, they must resemble fearsome dragons – and they certainly live up to the menace of their appearance.

When a ladybird larva comes across a fat and juicy aphid, it doesn't embrace her round the waist. It has hollow, sickle-shaped jaws which it sinks into the belly of its prey and literally sweeps it off its feet. I have watched the whole sinister drama through my magnifying glass and seen the greenfly hoisted clear of the ground so that its legs flap impotently in the air while the ladybird larva sucks away at its vital juices. When the meal is over and the victim has stopped struggling, the empty shell is cast aside so that the hollow jaws can capture its sister and drain away her life as well.

With such a rich and easy diet, it is small wonder that the ladybirds prospered and multiplied until the face of the earth seemed to be swarming with them. From our point of view, the result was far better than the scientists could have predicted because predatory ladybirds and their families sought out and destroyed aphids that it would have been uneconomic to wage chemical war upon.

But the ladybirds' very success was their own executioner. There was such an army of them that, when the battle was won and aphids were decimated, there was no longer enough food to sustain the victors. Their prime need was moisture, which was normally supplied by the body juices of their prey. When this was no longer available, they attacked flowers for the nectar although they are carnivorous. They even landed on man and were accused of 'biting' him although all the poor creatures were really doing was trying to get a drink by sucking the sweat globules upon his skin.

It didn't work, of course, so the wretched creatures had their virtue rewarded by a slow death from starvation. Some will survive, no doubt, to breed a nucleus which may provide free and efficient help for our farmers and gardeners next year. So I wish them well and I hope that they do not find their house on fire nor their babies gone. And, if they turn out to be the best control for insect pests again, I wish them better luck in maintaining a stable food supply.

20. Surplus Gamekeepers

In a current issue of a sporting magazine, the Situations Wanted column starts with a married man aged thirty, with three children, who wants to become a trainee gamekeeper. It is followed by a request from a single man who has just completed his O level in Zoology. He also wanted to be a trainee gamekeeper. He says he is 'very fit, hardworking and willing to go anywhere'.

Another applicant, single, and with three years' office experience wants to exchange life in the smoke and grime for the wide open spaces of the secluded countryside.

My own correspondence confirms that such pipe dreams are not rare. Scarcely a week goes by without school leavers writing to see if I can get them a job learning the trade of managing a shoot, while factory and office workers are mad keen to escape from the rat race to what they believe to be a saner life.

Most of them have romantic fantasies about what gamekeepers really do. They think they dress in smart plus-fours and stroll around the countryside with expensive shot guns under their arms, and a well-trained spaniel at their heels. The popular idea is that so far as his beat is concerned, the keeper's word is law.

Sadly, I have to destroy such illusions. Keepers' lives are not like that. The real thing entails being out in all weathers and at all hours.

Pheasants are the most stupid birds I know and are hell bent on roosting just where a fox can easily get them. If they escape the fox (largely because keepers get there first), they roost where they are most obvious to poachers who knock them off on moonlit nights.

Dealing with poachers nowadays is not the romantic job it was when I was a boy. Fifty years ago, there were conventions about what was and what was not permissible. Everybody fought by Queensberry rules and provided the gamekeeper was useful with his fists, he was respected, so that neither he, nor his adversary, got worse than a bloody nose.

Modern gangs have no scruples about putting the boot in. Knives are common and even guns are by no means rare. Glamour about protecting property against human predators is pretty illusory.

When I was young, my keeper friends were brilliant livestock keepers. The pheasant eggs were hatched by broody hens and reared in coops in open fields. It was tough work because good keepers literally camped out with their charges from May until the young pheasants went into the woods in autumn.

If you like the open air life, it has advantages, but things are different now. Modern keepers hatch eggs in incubators and rear chicks under infra-red lamps, as mass producing poultry breeders do. It is unskilled work compared to days gone by.

Worst of all, the type of employer has changed over the years. A

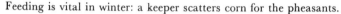

Feeding is vital in winter: a keeper scatters corn for the pheasants.

generation ago, most keepers worked directly for a family who had owned land for years, sometimes centuries, and respected not only the game that lived there, but people and wildlife too. Although it may sound feudal by modern standards, most of the men I grew up with enjoyed partnerships with their bosses which were welded into bonds of friendship.

Nowadays, most estates are leased to shooting syndicates whose members are first and last businessmen. They have made a pile of brass and the shoot is often paid for as a business expense. It is a status symbol to have a gun in a shoot, but such men, far from appreciating the whole pattern of the countryside, rarely visit it except in the shooting season.

Many of them would not know a bulrush from a bullfinch. They run the whole enterprise on business lines and expect their keeper to deliver the goods in the shape of pheasants and they don't care how he does it. He can destroy badgers, cats, hawks and owls, so long as he is successful. If he fails, they sack him, and his job has less security than a football manager.

It is obviously unfair to generalise because there are some good employers among syndicate shooters, just as there were baddies in the ranks of the old landowners. But modern trends make it harder and harder to find jobs that match with the visions most youngsters seem to have, and my advice to them is to work hard enough to become good shoot owners themselves, instead of unhappy keepers working for bad bosses.

21. The Infernal Combustion Engine

A sad sight in the autumn is the number of hedgehogs I see squashed on the road. The snag is that, when the hedgehog hears the car approaching, his natural instinct is to curl up in a ball for protection. If he had continued on his way across the road instead, the chances are that he would have escaped sudden death.

Nature endowed him with sharp prickles which cover him completely when he rolls himself into a ball, and gives him almost as good protection as a suit of armour. No modern engineer could have designed it more efficiently.

Each individual prickle is shaped rather like a hockey stick, with the short blunt end set under the skin. When the hedgehog is walking about, and his skin is loose, the prickles are slack and can point comfortably in any direction. But when the animal is alarmed and rolls himself into a ball, his skin is stretched tight so that the blunt end of the prickles, corresponding to the blunt end of the hockey stick which hits the ball, is pressed tightly between his skin and his body. This makes the prickles stand erect and firm so that touching them is like catching hold of a pin-cushionful of sharp needles.

Foxes get over the problem by nudging the hedgehog with their noses until he is on his back. He can only stay tightly curled by keeping his muscles flexed so that, the moment he relaxes, it is possible for the slender snout of a fox to slide through the prickly opening. Too late, the victim tenses his muscles again, but the tender snout is in the winning spot as surely as if it were the thin end of the wedge.

It is only a matter of time before the hedgehog has to take another breather and relax again, giving enough space for the snout to penetrate a fraction further. At last, the fox can take a grip of the tender under-fur and all is lost. A sharp pinch and a vicious shake and the hedgehog unfolds to make a tasty supper.

By comparison, motor cars are all brawn and no brain. They simply steamroller over any hedgehog which rolls up in their path. They don't just slaughter what they need as food, and I have even seen drivers who do not bother to take evasive action when road conditions leave them all the room they need to avoid catastrophe.

One reason that October is a particularly bad time of year for hedgehog road casualties is that they are about to hibernate for the winter. The chief factor that determines their chances of survival is the amount of body fat they have managed to accumulate. Although you might not think that you use up much energy while you are asleep, the fact is that every breath you take needs muscular effort to expand and contract your lungs.

So during the course of a winter's sleep, hedgehogs use up energy which is supplied by breaking down fat. By the end of winter, animals will die if they have not started with adequate reserves of fat.

Young born late in the season haven't a ghost of a chance from the start. Adult hedgehogs and those born early in the season behave as if they know how vital it is for them to accumulate fat reserves large enough to carry them through bad weather.

They come out early in the evening, and chobble up grubs and worms and snails as if they know that their lives depend on successful hunting. Which they do. They are particularly common in town gardens, where there are lots of bushes and shrubs for cover, and lawns and flower beds to harbour succulent worms, slugs and beetles. Large fields and the amount of chemical pesticides used by farmers mean that there are often fewer hedgehogs per acre in the country than there are in towns.

22. Protected – But Inadequately

Having written about the cause of the otter (*see* Nos. 9 and 18), I am delighted that the good wishes I expressed then have already come true. It was announced this week that an order before Parliament has added the otter to the list of Protected Species that are given total protection under the Conservation of Wild Species and Wild Plants Act. This is because the otter is among the creatures in serious danger of extinction.

The otter's inclusion is the result of an objective survey which has

A very fine otter on the river bank.

been carried out by members of the Mammal Society and Nature Conservancy Council and other scientists into the number of otters which still survive. It has been particularly difficult to do this because otters are among the shyest and most elusive of wild animals.

I spend more time than most in quiet and secluded places at all hours, but I can count on the fingers of one hand the number of times I have seen wild otters undisturbed. The first and most memorable was just as light was fading, on a superb summer's night, about a mile upstream from Montford Bridge in Shropshire.

A bitch otter was playing and diving with two cubs, rolling in the water and chasing each other's tails, in line astern, until they looked like a single miniature Loch Ness monster. I watched them until my eyes stood out on stalks, in a vain effort to pierce the gloom, and the picture will be etched into my mind for as long as I live.

Few of the scientists who have been carrying out the census of otter population have been so lucky and many of them have never seen a wild otter at all. They have accumulated their evidence by patrolling river banks at regular intervals, looking for footprints in the mud and 'spraints' or droppings. Otters are inveterate wanderers, often travelling for miles in the night, up or down stream. They communicate with each other by leaving spraints on prominent stones, as town dogs mark their passage on lamp posts and street corners.

Regular scientific observation, over a long period, gave an accurate assessment of the numbers of otters using the stretches of river covered by the naturalists. Otter hunters also helped in the work by making available the records they had kept, often for more than half a century. These recorded the number of otters their hounds had found, the number they had killed and the number that had got away.

Analysis showed how the population had varied over the years and the scientists were interested to discover that, despite continuous hunting for generations, it was well into this century before numbers began to slump. Over the last twenty or thirty years numbers decreased, and recently most hunts cooperated by recording the number of finds but calling off their hounds before they killed the otter.

Banning hunting, by putting the otter on the protected list,* will certainly help matters, but more positive steps are still essential. A

---

* Although the otter is now protected in England and Wales, Scotland is not yet as civilised and otters may still be slaughtered there.

great many otters have died of poison by catching prey that was already suffering from the effects of poisonous pesticides still used in agriculture. So it is vital to tighten up the law controlling poisons being allowed on the land. This would help other wildlife at the same time.

Suitable areas of riverside should be banned from walkers and fishermen and kept as reserves where otters could rest in peace and breed.

Most difficult of all is the control of people who still kill otters surreptitiously in spite of the law. There are still gamekeepers who believe their mission in life is to kill any creature with canine teeth, or bird with hooked bill like hawks and owls, lest they kill a pheasant or wild duck that their masters want to shoot, or just fish they wish to catch.

Otters are such slaves of habit that they follow the traditional paths of their ancestors and once it is seen where an otter goes, it is not only simple to trap him but a trap kept set in the same spot will catch every otter that follows him. Such people are almost impossible to catch since they set their traps on private property and visit them secretly when no one else is about.

There is even a loophole in the Conservation of Wild Species Act because exceptions are made for 'owners or occupiers who can justify that they acted to prevent damage to their property'. My opinion is that the onus should be on them to keep their stock secure.

So the present protection is no more than a step in the right direction. If the otter is to survive as a viable species, it will be necessary not simply to give it legal safeguards (which cannot yet be enforced), but to educate those who destroy its security by disturbance or think they have the right to exterminate everything to preserve extra pheasants or fishes for their amusement.

23. A Flirter Fills The Pram

Strangers might think that old Bill's missus was a glutton for exercise. She was often seen, at crack of dawn, pushing her pram down the most unlikely looking country lane, several miles from home. She was obviously a dedicated keep-fitter, people thought. But it was not the exercise that kept Bill's missus so lithe and healthy; it was the quality of grub she cooked.

When she left home before first light, her baby was sleeping snugly in the bottom of the pram. On her return, an observant onlooker might have noticed the kid was perched high enough to make the pram cover bulge over the sides. The infant was lying on a pile of pheasants, so well-concealed by the mattress that the most suspicious copper never raised his eyebrows.

Bill and his missus were the perfect partnership. He was the best shot I ever saw with a catapult ('flirter' he called it) and he loved to go out for an hour on moonlit nights because it helped, he said, if you could get your pheasant silhouetted against the moon!

He once told me he'd shot with the Earl of Dudley for more than twenty years. 'But he never found out,' he added.

When he'd got enough to eat, he hid them in a convenient ditch and, surprise, surprise, his missus 'happened' to pass the spot when she took the kid for his pre-breakfast walk.

I learned most of my natural history from chaps like Bill. They were an asset to the countryside and had forgotten more practical natural history than the blue-stocking boffins can ever learn at their dull laboratory desks.

Even if Lord Dudley had caught him red-handed, I doubt if he would have minded very much because most estates tolerated a few local characters 'knocking off' the odd rabbit or pheasant for the pot. Those who were caught and hauled up before the 'beak' were usually fined no more than a pound or thirty bob.

Things are very different now. Real poachers, the chaps who can read the countryside as clearly as a book, are almost extinct. They have been replaced by sneak thieves with rifles who park their cars in quiet lanes, pick off as many feeding pheasants as they can and are miles away before any keeper who hears the shot can get anywhere near.

The latest figures to be released by the Game Conservancy indicate that the cost of rearing a pheasant exceeds four pounds, so that intensive poaching is a really serious loss. Modern poachers treat their activities as a commercial enterprise and many of them operate in gangs and will not hesitate to rough-up anyone who interferes with them.

A local farmer owns a large, flat field next to the main road and, looking out of his window one Sunday morning, he saw eight men with greyhounds and lurchers walking across the field in a straight line. It was obvious they were looking for hares to course, so he took out his tractor and went over to drive them off. He got a pretty rough reception. They told him, in no uncertain terms, that they would pull him off his tractor and kick his ribs in.

None of the old-fashioned poachers of my day would have sunk to that level. They regarded poaching partly as a craft and partly as a sport. If they were caught, they reckoned to have lost the game. So the approach of a keeper was the signal to run for it, not to stand and fight.

That was where the skill came in. Chaps like Bill knew every ditch and hollow and it was second nature to them never to get silhouetted against the skyline. They literally seemed to melt away, as intangible as shadows.

Instead of trying to be neither seen nor heard, the moderns seem to seek publicity and some of the media are stupid enough to pander to them.

One man, who had been summoned for poaching deer, brought a six-inch nail with him and stuck it through the lobe of his ear. He then nailed himself to a wooden post outside the police court. If I'd been in charge, I would have left him to it, to tear himself free as best he could, but everyone rallied round as if he were the victim of an accident. The police surrounded him with a screen, and called the fire brigade to cut off the nail where it entered the wood. They took him to hospital to have the self-inflicted wound dressed instead of leaving him to ponder on his folly.

Full marks, therefore, to the magistrates at Shrewsbury who recently slapped on fines totalling £1937 on a gang of poachers who were caught killing deer with dogs in Attingham Park, which joins the A5 where it crosses the River Severn.

I know the game warden who had to examine the deer and he said their haunches had been so mauled they looked as if they had almost been eaten alive. Dogs cannot kill a deer cleanly as they could a hare, so it is a viciously cruel way of killing a deer, but the price of venison is so high that nothing but the toughest treatment will stamp out such cruelty.

24. Swansong

A stranger arrived on the doorstep the other day with a swan tucked under his arm. It was a magnificent bird, as white as TV washing powder, with a long powerful neck, designed for feeding deep under water and a vice of a bill that commanded respect.

My visitor said that he was a farmer and that he had found the great bird 'stuck' in the muckheap at the back of his cow shed. When he extricated it, it showed no signs of trying to fly away or even to stand up and walk. It simply squatted on the ground as if it were paralysed.

Birds as large and strong as swans simply do not get stuck in mire unless there is something seriously wrong with them, so the farmer thought of taking it to the vet. Then he thought again. Vets cost hard cash and he knew I have a pool where it would be safe from attack by foxes, so he turned up here with it.

I examined it carefully. Overhead electric pylons are real killers of such slow-flying birds. I have had several brought in to me, including a rare Bewick's swan, which had shattered a wing in the collision and had to have the broken part amputated. She recovered and lived happily here for years although she was never again able to fly.

But I could find no injury to this mute swan. He was a huge male, or cob, and he hissed in fury when I touched him. When I had confirmed that he had no bones broken, we took him down to the pool and gently launched him on to the water.

I watched particularly for the carriage of his neck. Many swans, nowadays, carry their necks lying partly along their backs, so that their heads seem to rear from their centre of gravity like the spindle of a wheel. It is a very bad sign, for birds so afflicted are doomed to die a slow and painful death. There is no known cure.

Sadly, our new patient showed these symptoms and eventually succumbed. Overhead pylons are no longer the greatest threat to the swans that beautify our rivers and lakes. The latest cause of death is slow lead poisoning, and one of the first symptoms is this peculiar carriage of the head and neck.

The mute swan displays his beauty.

The main cause is careless fishermen. Recent post mortems on 206 dead swans have proved that more than half of them died from lead poisoning. The cause is the lead shots that fishermen use to weight their lines to get the baited hooks down to the level where their quarry hides. Sometimes the birds pick up a baited fish hook complete with broken line and swallow the lot. It passes down the neck and enters the gizzard where grit is kept as part of the process of digestion. When the lead shot is eroded and ground to dust, it passes into the body so that the victim dies unpleasantly of lead poisoning.

Swans have broad bills and long necks so that they can reach deep into the lake and sift through the mud on the bottom, blowing out the fine grit and retaining solid particles that feel like corn or beetles. Discarded lead shot, chucked into the water and left in the mud, obviously feels like grains of corn or tiny water snails when sifted from the mud by the bill.

The split lead shot used to weight fishing lines is not the only danger. Years ago the Americans discovered that a high percentage of their wild duck were also dying of lead poisoning. This was not caused by fishermen but by duck shooters who lined the banks of lakes, shooting at duck over the water as they flew off or came in to land.

This caused such havoc among waterfowl that strenuous efforts are being made to persuade the manufacturers of shot gun cartridges to use steel balls instead of lead shot in their ammunition.

The English countryside is weekly littered with tens of thousands of plastic cartridge cases that do not disintegrate in the wet but are virtually indestructible. I have some in my study that have been chewed by deer and farmers suffer damage to their cattle and sheep from the same cause. Plastic string used for tying straw bales is just as bad.

So I am pessimistic about the chances of persuading fishermen and shooters to use better alternatives, even though it would be much safer for our wildlife. They prefer to stick to cheap lead shot though the sight of our innocent bird literally wasting away to inevitable death should have melted the hardest heart.

25.   The Old Cow Beats The Weatherman

The birds in our wood can't make up their minds whether to fall in love or not, despite the fact that we have just had St Valentine's Day. Most years, the herons arrive around Christmas, give or take a day or so. But the frost was too hard for comfort and the first skitter of snow made their tree tops too precarious for comfort so they went away again, deciding love in a snow storm was not for them.

The fact that they didn't come at their usual time around Christmas supports the country belief that birds and even plants can foretell weather. Greater accuracy than the weathermen on the radio would not be hard to achieve because their doleful tales of doom and destruction, the first time some old lady spins her car to a standstill, shake my faith in later forecasts that there will be drifts to stop a tank.

Lots of countrymen seem to be able to smell a storm on the wind long before it arrives, although they are incapable of explaining how they do it. My wife believes that when she sees cows lying down in a field there will soon be rain. I posed the idea to several scientists who sniffed with scorn and said it was rubbish.

'Storms', they said, 'are associated with barometric pressure and wind direction.' If scientists with ocean weather stations and radio communications can't foretell a shower of rain, they were certain that cows in a field couldn't.

A neighbouring farmer, on the other hand, is a first class cowman. Common Market green pounds and politicians more interested in urban votes than rural prosperity haven't put him out of business yet. So I asked him.

'Old Daisy, in the end stall, was infallible,' he said. If he went into a cow pasture to call up the herd for milking, he reached for his mac if Daisy was lying down. She likes her comfort and can't bear lying on wet grass. So she keeps her bed dry by lying on it before it rains, but not after. I have more faith in such first-hand observations than in the blathering of boffins.

Stories of huge crops of berries before Christmas foretelling a hard winter do less to convince me. Whatever the weather is going to be, it is impossible to get a big crop of fruit if the weather wasn't right for the blossom in the previous spring. So, in my view, crops of fruit and berries may be a good indication of what the weather was like in the past but it is only coincidence if they also foretell the future.

The herons are not the only visitors who have paid us a fleeting visit and then walked out on us. Two pairs of Canadian geese flew in a couple of weeks ago with a fanfare of loud trumpetings to herald their arrival. Last year, two pairs nested on the island in the pool and it was obvious that the birds this year, probably the same as last, had every intention of staking a claim before the accommodations got over-crowded.

Like the herons, they seem to have a low opinion of our hospitality. As soon as the pool froze over, they decided that they knew of more attractive quarters and flew away.

From the wild ducks' point of view, this was a pretty unfriendly act. There are always foxes where there is woodland and the ducks protect themselves from surprise attack by preventing a patch of water freezing by swimming around in it continuously. It must be hard work, despite the fact that they operate a shift system to share out the labour. Such powerful birds as Canadian geese mucking in as feathered ice-breakers would spread the load.

Although most animals and birds modify their timetable to suit the weather, it is astonishing how accurately they work to the calendar. Miss Roedoe, my tame roe deer, produced a kid each year in May. It was helpless and tiny so that its only chance of surviving attack by foxes was to rely on concealment.

It so happens that bracken comes into leaf very suddenly at about the time roe kids are born, but young bracken shoots are tenderly suscept-ible to frost, although the plant seems such a tough weed. So, if there was a frost in the air at the time Miss Roedoe was due to drop her kid, there was real risk that the bracken where she would normally hide it might be stricken down by frost. At those times, the kid might be born anything up to a week after the normal date. Was it luck, did the mother foretell a hard spring when she mated the previous summer, or is there some means by which she can delay birth when conditions are unfavourable?

Countrymen believe wild creatures can foretell the weather, while scientists say it is rubbish. I don't know, but on the whole I would prefer to lay my bets on countrymen against theories out of books.

26. Jac(k) Falls For A Cracker

As I've recounted in No. 3, a most delightful waif landed on our doorstep about a year ago. We named him Jac(k) because he was an orphan muntjac deer which had been sent to me to rear on the bottle. Young Jac thrived on bottles of milk and shared the study with the dogs and me for some months.

As he grew up, he wandered the paddock to graze sweet grass and clover there, and I fixed him up with an enclosure of about an acre of woodland and turf to prevent him wandering into danger.

Although he seemed happy and remained friendly with the dogs and me, I felt it was an unnaturally lonely life for him. If only I could find him a mate, his happiness would be complete.

It was easier said than done. Many of my friends are naturalists and some of them either keep muntjac or have to control them in areas where they are not welcome. The nearest Jac got to getting a mate was a young wild male which we thought was a female when we caught him and didn't discover our mistake for some months because we refused to risk frightening him by an examination. He had to go when we did find out because the risk of two males fighting in an enclosure from which the loser could not escape was too great.

So Jac has led a bachelor existence for the past year – until this week. A friend in Shropshire, who had bottle-reared a female, has been posted to another job. He was faced with the alternative of finding Cracker a new home or setting her free in woodland where she might easily be shot in mistake for a fox which is about the same size.

He promised to bring her over one day last week, but the telephone rang at breakfast time and it was my friend to say he had had a disaster. He had caught Cracker easily enough because she trusted him. She had such a shock when he thrust her into a strange travelling crate that she slipped from his hands, gave one mighty leap and jumped clean over the fence into the open woodland outside.

A passing dog saw her and gave chase and bowled her over. She was travelling so fast that he couldn't hold her so she slipped from his jaws

The muntjac has the freedom of the woods.

and disappeared into the wood. Her owner was sick with worry. He telephoned me to say he would not be coming and that he feared his favourite was done for.

An hour later, he telephoned again. He had managed to locate her in a thicket of bramble and recapture her with a net. He still didn't know the extent of her injuries, but said he would bring her over as I have better facilities for caring for injured animals than he has.

As soon as they arrived, we lifted her gently from the travelling crate and examined each leg to see if it was broken. One hindleg had been badly mauled by the dog but otherwise we could find no serious injury.

I had put a deep bed of soft straw in a small shed and darkened the window with a thick sack. Shock is the greatest killer of wild animals which are injured in such circumstances, so I left her alone for a full twenty-four hours.

Then I crept up to her shed, talking to her very quietly, so that she wasn't surprised by my arrival, and opened the door with bated breath. I feared she would be dead or, at least, completely crippled. To my delight, she was very much alive.

I left the door open so she could go outside into a grassy run next to the enclosure where Jac lives. She is much tougher than she looks.

Next day she and Jac were pacing up and down opposite sides of the fence obviously falling in love. So I opened another gate to let her join him in his large enclosure.

They have settled down as if she'd lived there all her life. Jac comes to me for titbits but Cracker isn't quite bold enough for that yet. I suppose she still remembers how her own boss bundled her into a crate. But the greatest gift with which Nature endowed me is almost inexhaustible patience. I can wait, because the confidence of such a delightful sprite is well worth waiting for.

One day, I hope she and Jac will trust me enough to give them the complete freedom of the wood.

27. Off Target

The Socialist Left-wing tried to include a ban on fox-hunting, hare-coursing, beagling and stag-hunting in their Labour Party election manifesto. Why not fishing and shooting and ratting as well? If abolishing cruelty is their aim, it is difficult to believe that a fish's slow death by drowning, with a barbed hook stuck through its lip, is any better than something meeting a violent end in the midst of a pack of hounds.

Thousands of people go out every weekend in winter to shoot anything from fashionable (and expensive!) pheasant to humble wood pigeons, which farmers are delighted to let them shoot for nothing.

A flock of wild duck live on the pool in front of my study window and they delight us by coming up to the house to feed on the grain I put out. They also know no better than to fly off to surrounding pools and rivers where sportsmen wait for them with guns. Some of the lucky ones never come back. They meet instant death from a charge of shot without ever knowing what hit them. We get a lot of limpers too. Not all sportsmen are good shots – and if they were certain of getting everything they shot at, I suppose they wouldn't count it as 'sport'.

So many birds are wounded and limp home painfully to die. The chap who shot them out of range, or didn't aim quite straight, probably thought he missed them. What the eye doesn't see, the heart doesn't grieve over. But I see them. They come hobbling painfully home, with shattered legs or wounded wings and those that do get better have a long and agonising convalescence. Some will obviously never recover. They are either mopped-up by the foxes, or I put them out of their misery with a rifle.

So why has the Socialist Left-wing picked on just a few sports to ban? Is the simple answer that they really don't know what they're trying to ban? Few would doubt that they would all fit two left blue stockings better than a pink hunting coat. But I cannot believe it hasn't dawned on them that all blood sports are cruel. So why don't they include them all?

Perhaps they think the sports they have chosen are the pastimes of the idle rich. Perhaps cruelty doesn't enter into it except to whip up a nice spot of electioneering class hatred? Or perhaps they think that shooting men and fishermen are stupid and that it won't occur to them that their pastime is reserved for later?

I have news for them. More people hunt now than before the First World War and about a quarter of a million follow hounds every Saturday, on horseback, on foot and in cars. Many of them shoot or fish as well, so the chances of them not noticing are pretty slim.

The opponents of blood sports are not hampered much by logic. The Hare Coursing Bill, which almost became law, would not have abolished hare coursing! It would only have made it illegal to slip greyhounds after a hare from a leash simultaneously, so the winner could be judged. It would not have been illegal to loose greyhounds into the fields and allow, or even encourage, them to chase any hare that got up. The hare would surely have found it just as unpleasant to be caught by loose hounds as by hounds which are slipped together to run in competition.

So let's have less hypocrisy and decide who is to be clobbered. Is this inclusion in the manifesto just another attempt to score off any class that is unlikely to vote Socialist? Or to score a few urban votes from folk who know as little of the facts as the sponsors seem to?

If the object is a genuine desire to abolish cruelty, good luck to it provided it is honest enough to admit that it is the thin end of the wedge which will lever out the rest later.

But while they are at it, why stop at hunting and coursing? For every fox that is killed by hounds, thousands of cattle suffer the misery of being exported alive to uncivilised customers, who neither attend to their basic needs on the journey nor give them a decent death in the slaughter-house.

I have had first-hand experience of some of the sickening practices of factory farming, and few would eat veal who have seen calves reared in crates to produce it.

There has been enough fuss in recent times about Britons being caned in Saudi Arabia. 'If they go to a foreign land', we are told, 'they must abide by the laws of that land.' Quite so. But if the lily-livered gang who rule us had the guts of a timid hare, they would practise what they preach and make foreigners in our land abide by our humane animal slaughter laws, instead of allowing them to bleed the animals to death. Let's get a few priorities right.

28: Good Old-fashioned Hotache

The West Country recently hit the headlines by disappearing under a blanket of drifting snow. But we, in the Midlands, were gripped in no less discomfort by invisible iron-hard frost.

Every morning, I had to tumble out of bed twenty minutes before my normal time. That is how long it took me to hump buckets of hot water round to thaw the ice in the hens' drinking fountains. Eggs consist of 90% water – or so the boffins say – and, judging by how much the laying hens consume, I wouldn't doubt their word. Certainly I know of nothing which will make them go on strike more quickly than no water in their troughs.

By the time the hens were quenching their thirst, there was a queue of pigeons and blue tits, blackbirds and thrushes, lined up by the bird bath behind our resident robin. He is always the head of the line when anything is going for nothing and he is never shy of letting it be known that he thinks the service does not come up to four-star rating. He sits on the rim of the bath with his feathers puffed out, eyes narrowed to a malevolent slit, sulking because the hens have come higher on my bill of priorities.

Suitably chastened (and wanting my own breakfast), I waste no time on formalities. I clout the ice in the bath with a crow bar, lever it out, and slurp in a couple of buckets of water.

I know of no more uncomfortable occupation than breaking ice with a crow bar. The least layer of water on the fingers is frozen by the icy iron and clings like sticking plaster to a hairy arm. The flesh gradually goes numb with cold, after which the pain of thawing out brings back childhood memories of snowballing and 'hotache'.

After breakfast, I reckon to take the dogs round the wood – whatever the weather. Our soil is normally puggy clay which moulds itself to the cleated soles of my gumboots. Now it is frozen so hard that the ruts and humps provide the precise sensations that must spur Indian fakirs to visions of immortality when they lie on their beds of nails.

Yesterday, a grey squirrel was stupid enough to come down to earth to cross a ride too wide for the branches to span. He would normally have had a one-way ticket to eternity because the dogs are allowed to chase rats and squirrels which wreak havoc among small nesting birds. But, in common with their master, the dogs rate running over frozen woodland a pastime which holds few attractions.

Fly, my ancient lurcher, forgot in the heat of the moment that she is officially on the retired list, and streaked halfway across the clearing. Then, with a piercing yelp, she stopped in her tracks holding up her right foreleg and simpering for pity, like the mollycoddle she is. I had every sympathy. Walking gingerly over the rocky ruts has made my feet so tender that I hobble around, when I get up in the morning, as if the

Feeding very hungry ducks.

bedroom carpet were made of cobble stones.

But it's ône thing to endure a little temporary discomfort. It's another if you have to find food in these conditions. The hunk of fat outside my study window has been supplemented by other mammoth helpings outside the kitchen and the sitting-room. Blue tits and great tits, coal tits and marsh tits are tumbling over each other for a foothold that will let them bury their beaks in the life-giving food.

We have a resident population of feathered scroungers, headed by the robin, who regard our house as Easy Street. But most of the small birds around now are strangers who normally work hard for their living. They spend their days hopping about the woodland floor, turning over the leafmould in search of tiny beetles and spiders or other creepie-crawlies.

But the frost has glued the leaves into a solid carpet, far too strong to be torn apart by weaklings. Their bodies are so tiny it is almost impossible for them to retain life-giving heat through bitter nights. Occasional hard winters are Nature's way of controlling their surplus population.

Even large animals are feeling the pinch. The grass in our paddock and woodland rides is as brown as desert sand; horrible, withered, brittle rubbish which is hardly fit for pack-belly, far less for nourishment. The deer have bitten it down till it looks as if there is no chance it will perk up again, and produce the lush green pasture that makes summer in England so much more lovely than any foreign land.

Sensing my sympathy, the deer congregate in a forlorn, hunchbacked group on the woodland edge. Experience has taught them what a sucker I am for such sob sister stuff. I can always be counted on to go to the rescue with a bucket of corn I can't really spare.

29. Friction In The Countryside

Three years ago, my neighbour let his land to a syndicate shoot. He owns around a thousand acres of woodland and a thousand acres of farm.

At that time, I had a fine few badgers in my wood which I did all in my power to encourage and in April there was a sow badger with four cubs living in a sett about eighty yards from my study window.

Badgers do very little harm to shooting interests. If they happen to blunder across a pheasant's nest, they will probably eat the eggs, but this only happens accidentally and not because they hunt them out deliberately as foxes do. On the credit side, badgers bumbling about in the undergrowth disturb any pheasants roosting on the ground so that, next night, they take refuge in the treetops where they are safe from foxes.

So I was not particularly worried that my new neighbours would harm my badgers if they strayed on to the shoot, especially as badgers were legally protected.

The day the keeper called, my spirits slumped. 'I gather you are the man who harbours badgers,' he said, by way of introduction.

'Harbours' badgers. I didn't like the sound of that. My worse fears proved justified because, within weeks, I found evidence of badgers being caught in snares.

I arranged a meeting with the principal of the syndicate and explained I had been doing scientific work on badgers for years, that I was particularly fond of them and I would deem it a favour if he would see they came to no harm if they strayed on to his land.

No luck. He was a businessmen and didn't like predators which ate into his profits and, although it would be illegal to snare them, it was not illegal to snare foxes. If badgers got caught by mistake, too bad. So far as I was concerned, it was a declaration of war. If his pheasants strayed into my wood, too bad also. They would have a one-way ticket.

The upshot was that the syndicate have gone away to shoot else-where, though it has taken two years for the badgers to realise they can find sanctuary in my wood. There are now signs that the sett I made about eighty yards from my study window is occupied again. I have not seen the occupant but, judging by the size of the footprints in the mud, it is a last year's cub which will probably have to stay another year before it breeds.

I never go nearer than twenty or thirty yards from the sett because I am determined to take no risks of disturbing her – or him. But when it is light later at night, we should be able to see it cross the woodland rides when it sets out in search of food at dusk.

The badger sets out on his first prowl of the night.

The snag has been that the shoot was vacant again and the owner advertised it for letting to the highest tender. All sorts of people came to view it and it soon became obvious that we might have jumped from the frying pan straight into the fire. It was even rumoured among the locals that one 'gentleman' shot a deer while sizing up the prospects.

When the tenant was decided upon, the owner invited me to a meeting with the new syndicate and their keeper. It was a nail-biting moment for all of us. I have no doubt they would have heard what happened before but, in case nobody had told them, I said precisely what I had done and why.

We got on fine. The keeper was obviously a very professional chap who knew the job backwards and he assured me he had no designs on my badgers. His words carried conviction. I shall reciprocate by discouraging potential poachers or disturbance at my end of the shoot. His pheasants which stray on to my ground will be safe – and I am confident my badgers will come to no harm on his.*

The whole situation is typical of the frictions that often lead to worse neighbour relations in the countryside, where we live half a mile apart, than in towns where folk can't help getting under each other's feet.

One farmer I know is notorious for never keeping his hedges in trim. His cattle have always got out and trespassed on the next farm so there are always squabbles about the amount of food they eat. Folk in villages let their dogs wander where they like while the family is at work – and are surprised and hurt when they are shot at lambing time. Ditches that are allowed to get clogged up until they back-up and prevent those upstream from draining their land are a continual source of friction.

Perhaps, in comparison, my badgers are a minor niggle. But, looked at from the badger's point of view, the molehill really is a mountain.

* The full story is told in Phil Drabble's *No Badgers in my Wood*, published by Michael Joseph in November 1979.

30. Daft Ducks Give The Game Away

A mallard duck has laid a clutch of eggs under the shelter of a bush by our sitting-room window. She has laid an egg every day but two in the last fortnight and as soon as she has laid it, she covers the whole nest with leaves which have drifted into the corner during winter storms.

If she didn't take this precaution, she would never have completed the clutch because the crows, magpies and jays would steal every egg as fast as she laid it. Even so, she will be lucky to keep her precious eggs safe because she is such a slave to habit that she gives the game away as surely as any wages clerk who calls at the bank with his little black bag at exactly the same time every week. If she were human, a gang of thugs would lie in wait and cosh her for her cash.

Her one advantage is that her nest is cleverly hidden and if only her old man were bright enough to keep away, there would be nothing to alert prospective raiders that this was the site of treasure trove.

Unfortunately, mallard drakes are just plain stupid. The ducks visit their nest soon after dawn to lay a daily egg and they are always accompanied by their dutiful drakes who sensibly mistrust the motives and morals of rival drakes.

I happened to look out of the window first thing the other morning just in time to spot 'our' pair of ducks flying up from the pool, across the paddock to alight on the lawn. Next time I looked through the window, the drake was sitting by himself looking as bored as a husband wasting Saturday afternoon waiting for his missus outside the supermarket. Looking further round, I saw no less than four more drakes mooning away their time until their mates deposited an egg, covered the nest again and returned to the water.

So I got up a bit earlier next morning, and sure enough, I was in time to see them all leave the pool and disperse to the bushes and other thick cover around. The drakes settled down to wait in about the same

94

positions as the day before, and the ducks wandered off, apparently casually and at random.

But there was nothing casual about it. Their beady eyes searched incessantly for anything suspicious. They were as cunning in their efforts to keep the secret of their hiding place as any story book miser.

Just to amuse myself, I made a slight movement which was spotted by the duck on the lawn as easily as if I'd let off a gun. Without a moment's hesitation, she took wing and landed with a splash in the water. Although I waited another hour, she didn't return. Next day, I was careful not to give my game away. That was how I found the nest concealed by the window.

Eventually, our duck left to be greeted by her mate who chased her in a spiral love flight until they almost disappeared as specks in the sky. When they reached their ceiling, she peeled out of her routine, and returned to the pool, followed hot foot by the drake. He didn't give her a second respite but chivvied her round till he caught her and claimed the reward of his patience on the lawn and his efforts in the sky by mating her with caveman ardour.

I wonder if the chores of going shopping have similar benefits!

I have kept close observation on our nest, counting the eggs as they have been laid. The nest itself has none of the intricate woven structure of the nests of thrushes or robins. It is simply a depression scraped in the ground under the shrub so that it will act as a saucer and prevent the eggs rolling out and dispersing.

During the day when the birds are on the pool, there are no eggs to be seen. They are carefully covered with a blanket of leaves which the duck drags towards her with her bill each morning after she has laid.

When she had laid nine eggs, she stayed on the nest half an hour or longer and showed obvious signs of going broody and wanting to stay altogether to incubate the clutch. When she got off the nest and her mate came to greet her, her feathers puffed out and she wanted nothing to do with him. Although he didn't take 'no' for an answer, he had to chase her much higher and much further before she allowed him to mate her. Chivalry was obviously not one of his strong points.

Now she has completed her clutch of twelve eggs, she has feathered her nest. When she leaves it to bathe and feed, the eggs are not simply left covered with leaves to conceal them. They are covered with a warm soft eiderdown of feathers she has plucked from her own breast.

Only when her clutch is complete does she start to incubate them which ensures that all the ducklings will hatch on the same day so that they can be reared together. The eggs take twenty-eight days to hatch, not from when they were laid but from when the duck stops laying and goes broody. From then on, she will spend about twenty-three hours a day brooding them until they hatch. But her flamboyant drake waiting each morning to escort her to bathe and feed does draw attention to her secret and if a crow spots the nest as I did, all her labours will have been in vain and the crow will have egg for breakfast.

31. The Minkhounds Wreak Havoc

I am not the sort of dedicated do-gooder who tries to stop everything I do not enjoy myself. Horses hold no attraction for me and I have little in common with those who charge round the countryside yelling 'Yoicks' every time they see a fox.

If foxes were rare, I would do all in my power to make the sport illegal. As things are, I consider it no business of mine that others enjoy what I should find boring so I keep my thoughts to myself unless they annoy me directly, by trespassing on my land or disturbing threatened species. Otter hunting was quite different and I was delighted when otters were added to the list of protected species.*

So I find it very disturbing that some packs of otter hounds are hoping to hunt mink instead. Mink belong to the same family as ferrets but they are larger and stronger and far more agile. They are also even more bloodthirsty.

Fish are among their favourite prey, so any that escape from fur farms thrive best if they discover exactly the sort of river otters love. They do far more harm than otters because they prey on all sorts of birds, from domestic poultry to wildfowl, as well as song birds, fish and pheasants.

Like grey squirrels, mink are aliens which have settled here well, but they are a far greater threat to our wildlife than stoats, weasels or foxes or any other native predator. There is good cause to kill them and I would shoot, trap, poison or gas them by any means I could. But I would not hunt them for the simple reason that they choose to live in the places otters like, and it would be impossible to hunt mink without disturbing otters, which have more than enough to contend with as it is.

Changing fashions – and affluence – have a nasty habit of endangering the most unlikely creatures. Until the last war, falconry was an almost unknown sport in this country.

* See Nos. 9 and 22.

I used to know a man who rented the grouse shooting on the Long Mynd in Shropshire – but never shot a grouse or allowed anyone else to do so. He spent the late summer and autumn in an isolated gamekeeper's cottage in the heart of the moor and was joined by a few friends who congregated there from all over the world. Most of them were rich enough to spend weeks on end there and all were dedicated and knowledgeable falconers.

They used mostly gyr falcons and peregrines and their quarry was grouse. They had pointers and setters to find the birds, crouching in the heather, and a trained hawk would circle, like a buzzard, high overhead until the quarry was flushed. Then the hawk would 'stoop' in pursuit, reaching speeds of a hundred miles an hour in the attacking dive. Most often the grouse escaped by diving into thick cover but occasionally the falcon would triumph and strike it down in full flight.

A goshawk striking the lure.

It was by far the most spectacular sport I have seen and I was always delighted to be invited for a day as a guest. So few people had the time, money or expertise to engage in falconry that neither the hawk nor the grouse species were threatened.

Increased wealth and leisure have altered all that. All sorts of people with neither the knowledge nor facilities to keep hawks muscled in, and demand was such that prices rose and the robbing of nests threatened the survival of many species. Even Arab sheiks now offer four-figure sums for English peregrines.

So I am delighted to see new proposals to make it illegal to sell any British hawk that has not been bred in captivity and has a close ring on its leg to prove this. This will include everything from golden eagles to common kestrels.

It is reassuring that common sense really does prevail sometimes so that creatures like otters and hawks, in genuine need of protection, can be safeguarded without destroying a legitimate if controversial rural pursuit.

32. Ruthless Rabbits

Mad March hares are conspicuous by their absence this year. In normal years, one of my pleasures, in spring, is to sit by my study window to watch the hares disporting. (*See* No. 53.)

The hares around here seem to spend most of their winters in the warmth and safety of deep woodlands, from which they make their nightly expeditions to raid the local farmers' crops. Then, when the corn begins to sprout, they substitute the comfortable haven of woodland for the more exciting prospects of growing crops where the fact that they are more conspicuous loses some of the perils because the shooting season is finished.

Hares spell spring to me because when I see them playing hard-to-get at the edge of our wood, I know that all the other signs of spring are not far behind.

So when the other signs of spring arrived without the hares, I felt deprived and searched my mind for reasons. The most likely cause is rabbits. Stoats, foxes, dogs and men with guns may fill the minds of scatter-brained hares with visions of violent death, but the real niggers in the woodpile are more likely to be rabbits.

Whatever public image innocent bunnies may inspire, the harsh fact is that they are really little horrors. Buck rabbits have no inhibitions about eating their young. The does may not be aware that their passionate mates have murder in their hearts but they take instinctive precautions to nip disaster in the bud.

They leave the communal burrows before their time is up, dig a secret tunnel away from other rabbits, and produce their young in safety there. What the buck's eyes do not see poses no temptations so that there is a fair chance that the innocent young rabbits survive.

Hares have different techniques. The females have their young in the open and limit the risks of violent death by leaving each young leveret in a different form, or nest, which the mother only visits when it is time the young were suckled.

Unlike rabbits, which are born naked and blind, hares are born with their eyes open and fully furred. They simply rely on camouflage to keep them safe from harm. This works fine with stoats and foxes and other natural predators which only stumble on them by chance. But, when rabbits are thick on the ground, they graze the herbage closely and it is never long before they come across any young hares by accident.

Being as spiteful as many so-called 'harmless' creatures are, buck rabbits take it out on anything even weaker so that young hares would not be rated as an insurable risk in thriving rabbit country.

Just at the moment, we have rather too many rabbits in our wood and this is why I think I have seen so few hares this year. Myxomatosis, the killer disease which scientists predicted would wipe rabbits from the face of the earth, is not as lethal as predicted. When it was first introduced, in the 1950s, many believed that rabbits were doomed to extinction, but a few survived.

The next wave of the plague accounted for a slightly smaller proportion of the population until, when we had it in our wood last year, it wiped out less than half of them.

Scientists are busily engaged in producing an even more lethal strain (in spite of the fact that it would be illegal to spread it if they did) but I will put my shirt on rabbits still being in the running when the boffins are forgotten in their graves.

33.   Wildlife Pays The Price Of Progress

Over Easter, the ether was buzzing with news of thousands of tons of oil which threatened the Channel Islands' holiday industry by polluting the beaches. Last week, the City of York's water supplies were threatened because a poisonous chemical was swilled into the river during a farm fire. This week, the village of Panteg, near Pontypool, is up in arms about the disposal of an American chemical which is said to produce sterility in those who sniff it. Charming!

We must be out of our minds to allow such suicidal nonsense. Our politicians seem besotted with the dogma that no price is too high to pay to save hours of man's labour. An oil tanker five times as big as anything before presumably saves four captains and the best part of four crews when compared to five conventional vessels. Apart from the fact that the labour cost saved is illusory since redundant seamen have to be paid by someone, any disaster with such 'super' tankers is likely to be five times as bad.

It has been computed that twenty million pounds will not clean the beaches defiled by oil from the *Amoco Cadiz*. You could have hired a lot of crews for smaller vessels and still had change in your pocket from that.

Most of the outcry which arose from this disaster centred on the havoc it might cause by making beaches unpleasant to bathe from. Just as work has become a dirty word in our society, leisure is treated as the golden calf. I am more concerned about lingering deaths to sea birds than a few grubby marks on the dolly-birds' bikinis.

It is typical of our twisted sense of values that thousands of gallons of detergents were sprayed on the oil to break it up and make it sink before it could reach and foul the beaches. Once below the surface of the sea, it could be conveniently forgotten. As it sank lower, the fish would inhale it so that it would choke their gills, but no matter.

In the Ministry of Agriculture's List of *Approved Products for Farmers and Growers*, M.C.P.A. is recommended as a translocated herbicide. The List recommends that livestock be kept away for two weeks after use and that containers should be burned. Here a container has been turned into a wheat-feeder for pheasants by a keeper, and wild birds are joining the feast in complete ignorance.

My solution would be to minimise the risks by returning to smaller vessels and being utterly ruthless about setting fire to any vessels in serious danger of fouling the sea with oil, to avoid contaminating the water.

Last week, the focus shifted to York where there was danger that the deadly chemical Paraquat swilled by firemen's hoses from a farm fire would get into drains or ditches and contaminate the water. Paraquat is one of the chemical weedkillers sold to farmers to save the labour of old-fashioned cultivation. It is a persistent and deadly poison and instructions are carried on each tin, warning the farmer to keep his cattle off the land after spraying. There is no advice about how to protect wildlife!

The booklet issued by the Ministry of Agriculture about approved products for farmers and growers makes terrifying reading. It includes detailed instructions about the quality of protective clothing required before some of the substances should ever be handled. They include rubber gloves, boots, overalls and even a special respirator. It is still dangerous to eat some crops six weeks after spraying.

We have grown so blasé about the use of chemicals that the Ministry rat catchers go around with poisons instead of ferrets, and gas badgers instead of rats without raising much outcry from the public.

When rabies comes, there are plans to plaster the countryside with poison to eliminate the foxes which could spread it. At best, this is a prime example of shutting the stable door after the horse has gone. It might be more sensible to take preventive action against foxes and toughen laws against those who smuggle pets into the country while there is still time. But both courses might be politically unpopular – so neither has been adopted.

This week's instalment of stupidity is up to the standard of lemmings jumping to their doom over a cliff. The Panteg Environment Protection Society have had to take legal proceedings to halt what it claims are unpleasant and dangerous smells that permeate the area when waste chemicals are burned at a local factory. What an insane world we live in when we must form societies to protect humans and wildlife from industrial excrement, spewed out to save labour costs which, in turn, create unemployment.

But it is encouraging to realise that the results of such passionate campaigns have forced the bureaucrats to tighten up controls on some of the dangerous farm chemicals which wreaked havoc among our wildlife in the 1950s. Species that dwindled through poisonous pesticides are now recovering. Threatened plants and insects still beautify our countryside.

I am grateful that politicians are still sensitive to public pressure and there are still citizens prepared to supply it.

NB Phil Drabble's book, *No Badgers in my Wood*, covers the problem of chemical pesticides in more detail.

34. Change For Change's Sake

Nothing raises my hackles quicker than politicians messing about with my traditional way of life. I know what an acre looks like. I can visualise it quite clearly. It is a patch of ground approximately seventy paces square. When I am travelling around the country, I can look over the roadside hedges and assess the size of the fields I see in venerable English acres.

The bureaucratic jargon which advertises farms for sale in hectares might just as well be in Greek as far as I am concerned. It means nothing to me.

The size of a cow's udder gives me a good idea whether she is a good cow giving six or eight gallons a day or whether she is a scrubber, hardly capable of filling a two-gallon bucket. What the equivalent would be in litres, I neither know nor care.

Nor have I become reconciled to the worthless washers that pass for money these days. I regard them as a device, dreamed up by shifty politicians, to deceive me about the rate of inflation. If you subconsciously convert the present price of a pint of ale or pound of steak into honest £.s.d., you cannot but agree.

The same goes for holidays. Christmas, Easter and Whit, with their seasons calculated from saints' days, as they have been since we first grew civilised, were good enough for me. So far as I am concerned, you can keep the new-fangled May Day holiday, for I have no intention of celebrating any Communist festival.

Last Monday, which was fine at home, the air above the fields throbbed with the throaty roar of tractors on full bore and reeked of diesel fumes. It has been a cruelly cold, late spring and, whenever there are a couple of dry days, it is vital to get machinery on the land.

Farmers are paid for what they produce. There are no contingency bonuses to cover hard lines and if their crops fail through bad management, bad weather or stupid politicians trying, like King Canute, to turn the tide of supply and demand, too bad. The farmers carry the can. So, when the weather is right, and the soil in fine fettle, tractors rumble out whether it is Sunday or weekday to get the job done while the going is good.

Many farms in our area are still family businesses, handed down generation after generation, from father to son. Nobody bothers about overtime or double time for bank holidays any more than wives want paying extra for washing up the supper things.

One of my neighbours works a shift system with his sons, so that one continues ploughing whilst the others eat, and they relieve him for his meal as soon as they have finished. Their tractor starts up at half past six or seven and never stops running, except for refuelling, until long after dark. 'Headlight' corn we call it, for when my generation slow up in the evening, beams of light still flicker across the fields at the edge of the wood. When they make a profit, they have earned it.

At the beginning of the week, I joined the metallic symphony. I was narked that Englishmen should sink to the level of celebrating a Communist holiday. I normally work hard for my living because, like farmers, I only get paid for what I write. If my pen runs dry, I shall be the first to go hungry and then thirsty. I have practical priorities.

I was determined to make my protest, not by going on a demo and shaking my fist, but by doing twice as much work in a day as bearded demonstrators could.

So I trundled out my old tractor from the shed and ministered to her needs with loving care. I filled her with diesel and checked her oil levels and tyre pressures. Her radiator leaks a bit, so that was checked as well.

She is a trusty old steed which first coughed into life over twenty years ago in 1957. I have had her for fourteen years and she has never let me down. Of course, she doesn't do as much work as modern tractors do – and, anyway, I am too old to keep pace with my young neighbours. Too much of my time is spent pushing my pen, but neither of us is too bad for our vintage!

Last autumn, I cleared a patch of scrub in the wood which has been waiting for a suitable spell of fine weather to allow me to cultivate it and sow it with grass seed for the deer to graze. The soil is cold and clammy clay. If I got on it too soon, it would compact as solid as concrete so that grass seed would stand no chance of thrusting in its roots.

The beginning of this week was just right. I hitched a set of disc harrows and pounded them over the rough ground for hour after hour. When they had cut the soil into a fine tilth, I hitched on a roller instead and levelled it down to a seed bed.

When I had done, I was stiff and sore and the old tractor creaked from doing twice a normal day's work. I wallowed in the luxury of a hot bath, cocking a snook at politicians and mentally unfurling my Union Jack.

35. Don't Underrate The Dogs

Stuffy scientists claim animals do not 'think'. They say their reactions to situations are automatic and people who claim their dogs or cats are capable of constructive thought are confusing intelligence with instinct.

My instinct is to kick such bench-bound boffins in the seat of their pants for their arrogance. My dogs – and I expect your dogs too – could teach most of these clever dicks that man has no monopoly of constructive thought.

The point was brought home to me when I got a rude awakening last week. Belle, my Alsatian, has the run of the yard and paddock at night so unwanted guests would not find Welcome on the mat if they were stupid enough to open the gate from the drive.

There is a brick-built outhouse where she can sleep when not actively engaged in guarding the yard and house. I have fitted it up with a warm bed raised out of the draughts, and any other doggy mod. cons. that occurred to me. In theory, it should be just the mixture of comfort and liberty that is paradise for dogs.

In practice, she appears to be rather status-conscious. Although she spends the night free to roam outside, she spends the day with my pointer, Tick, and me. When I am working in my study, they lie asleep at my feet. When I go out in the woods, they come too. And when I join my wife by the fire in the evening, the dogs keep the hearth rug warm.

Belle obviously classes herself as a house dog and, however comfortable her sleeping quarters are, she thinks she should have a more impressive address than 'The Yard'. I fail to see why she should be so upstage. My study is a later addition to the house. It is outside the back door – in the yard as well!

The door does not open with a knob but a handle in the form of a lever. Belle watched me open it with my elbow when I was carrying a tray of coffee – and with no teaching from me, the penny dropped. She found out for herself that all she had to do to get in was to rear up on her

109

Tick and Belle sharing the same bed.

hind legs and pull down the lever with her front paw. She leaned against the door to do so and it naturally flew open.

It solved her problems of having more desirable sleeping quarters. As soon as she has finished the meal I give her just before I go to bed, she opens the study door for herself and settles down on my chair!

The boffins might say, 'So what? She didn't find out how to open the door by using her intelligence, but by the accident of leaning up against the door to push it, which is instinctive, and pressing down the lever without realising what she did.'

Right, then, but what about learning to get out of the study? If she jumped up against the door to push it, by instinct, she might depress the lever, but that wouldn't open the door because it will only open from the inside, towards her. But she soon discovered how to hook down the lever and pull it towards her, so she can now get out as easily as she can get in. If scientists deny that that is intelligent, they should get mangled in their computers.

The practical result is that the dogs can now get through any of our doors unless we actually turn the key in the lock.

The day after she cracked the secret, she came out of the study at five in the morning and burgled the back door. She went straight to the kitchen where Tick sleeps, opened the door and dug her out of bed. By now they were both feeling a bit above themselves, so they came upstairs and burst into our bedroom, leaped on to the bed to demonstrate what clever dogs they were, and licked us until we had to disappear under the bedclothes for protection.

If I hadn't succumbed to their demands to go out for a walk – it was a perfect morning – they might have learned to pull the bedclothes off!

Anyone who has owned a working dog will have seen him profit by experience and use his intelligence to put it to good use. For over twenty years, my hobby was ratting and my two Staffordshire bull terriers each killed over a thousand rats in a year, and a hundred in a day. By anybody's yardstick, that is a lot of rats.

Rats frequently escaped by running up the corner inside a barn and disappearing into the roofspace. There wasn't much time to grab them, and the dogs sometimes accelerated so fast they caught the rat but couldn't stop before colliding with the wall. It was surprising how soon they learned to tip the rat off balance so they had time to slow up and nab the quarry before it recovered its balance to climb the wall.

Tick has a musical ear and knows which tune ends the television News at Ten and that I feed her then before going to bed. So she gives me no peace the moment the music starts.

Animals are not the foolish automatons the scientists would have us believe, and if they think they are, they should not judge others by their own yardstick.

36.   A Leech Took Me For A Sucker

Letitia Lonsdale might have been Boadicea or the Queen of Sheba or any other famous woman in history – if only she had lived long enough ago. As things turned out, she ended up as my school matron.

Don't let that fool you into thinking she was insignificant. Anything but. She was tall and willowy, with hypnotic eyes and an aristocratic nose. Everyone from my head master, whom I disliked, to the captain of rugger, whom I also disliked, was terrified of her. So it may seem strange that she was very kind to me. This could have been simply because I was always a bit of a rebel, getting into endless trouble.

It turned out extremely useful for me because, when things got too hot, I used to retreat to Letitia's surgery where she doled out opening medicine, closing medicine, bandages and lint. Anyone rash enough to pursue me up there walked into a hornets' nest. She drew herself up to her full height, glared at any intruder, from master to head prefect, and after an interminable silence, demanded coldly, 'Yes? What is it?'

School gaffers tend to be big fish in little pools, with an inflated idea of their own importance, but the brashest of them know when they are licked. They stuttered and mumbled and slunk away defeated.

Letitia was no chicken. She was eventually stricken with pneumonia and carted away to the school 'san'. It was in the days before antibiotics and, despite the chaplain's efforts at morning prayers, it was feared she would die. The salvation came from a surprising source. Leeches.

I gather that some boxers still use leeches to suck away the congealed blood of a black eye, but at the time it seemed to be scraping the barrel a bit to put leeches on Letitia's high-bred brow. They did the trick though. She weathered the crisis and slowly began to pull through.

In the old days, leeches were kept for sale in every chemist's shop. The huge elegantly-shaped jars filled with sparkling coloured water in modern chemists' windows were not there originally for decoration.

113

They were once used by apothecaries to display the leeches which could then be selected to relieve patients of a little blood.

Letitia was far more modern. When she recovered enough to cock a critical eye round her private ward, the first thing she saw was a jar of leeches. They were as revolting as sinuous slugs, undulating round their watery cage like tiny Loch Ness monsters.

'Take those foul things out of my room,' she ordered, 'and give them to Drabble. They're just the thing for him.' So her leeches, in a tightly-screwed honey jar, were delivered to my study.

I was flattered beyond belief, to be honoured as custodian of the creatures that had saved Letitia's life. So I took them promptly to the biology lab and asked Bunny, the master, for practical advice. He was called Bunny because of his buck teeth and because his family was so large. If I had been a ferret, he couldn't have liked me less.

'What do you feed them on, sir?' I asked. 'Blood,' he barked. 'What sort of blood?' 'Any blood. Get on with your work.'

I took a frog from the laboratory store, held it belly uppermost, and reverently placed a leech on the fattest softest part. No go. The leech wasn't interested. So I took my flirter, as catapults were called, and shot a sparrow. I plucked him while he was warm and tried the leech on that. My luck was no better.

Very worried, it was my turn to snap back at Bunny. 'These creatures saved our matron's life – and they'll starve if we don't feed them. What sort of blood *do* they suck?'

With unrabbit-like ferocity, he snarled, 'Yours, boy. Yours. Try them on that.'

So I put the leech on the palm of my hand and watched him slide as smooth as a snail to a vein at the centre of the soft part of my forearm. All work stopped and the class gathered round, entranced, to watch the leech hanging from my arm with blood pulsating down it as if it were being milked by an invisible hand.

Filled by about an egg-cupful of blood, it hung limp like an Indian club. 'Get it off, boy,' squeaked Bunny. 'It's had enough. Get it off!'

Easier said than done. When I pulled it, it stretched like elastic so I eventually pinched it with a pair of tweezers.

Four hours later, I was still bleeding. Letitia's stand-in sent me to the doctor who had to stitch up a hole it had chewed in my vein.

'Who told you to put it there?' he asked. 'Bunny,' I replied.

'Well, you don't put a leech on like that. You put it in a test tube over a bony part that you can easily stop bleeding. Next time you see Bunny, tell him from me that he is a bloody fool.'

I did. Then I bolted for the sanctuary of Letitia's convalescent room. And the scar on my arm reminds me of it every time I have a bath.

NB This story was also told in Phil Drabble's book. *Of Pedigree Unknown*, published by Cassell in 1964 and re-issued by Michael Joseph in 1976.

37. Croakers Croak No More

My old friend Pat Welsh had forgotten more country lore than most countrymen know. This was surprising because he was born in the Black Country of Staffordshire and worked all his life down the pit – an unlikely school for rural knowledge. He was filled with the rare courtesy that stamps people 'gentlemen', whatever their background. His family migrated from Ireland towards the end of last century. So perhaps it was a touch of the Blarney Stone that gave him such a winning tongue.

One of his favourite sayings, during the sort of cold, wet spring we so often endure, was that there would be 'no warm weather till the corncrak crewed'.

The corncrake: drawing by J. H. Blackburn, published in *Birds from Moidart*, 1895.

JB *Corncrake*

The corncrak (or corncrake) was getting a rare bird by the end of the First World War, but Pat's memory spanned well into the last century: he died over twenty years ago. It is a brown bird, about as big as a partridge, with chestnut wings and paler below. Apart from the fact that it is now rare, you are unlikely to see it because it is a skulker. It creeps around in long grass and dense undergrowth and is shy of being seen.

As its name suggests, it is a craker (if not a crower). Its Latin name is *Crex crex*, which is a pretty accurate description of the noise it makes. It repeats the monotonous call again and again, from different parts of the field so that it could be mistaken for a flock of birds singing a chorus or an exceptionally clever ventriloquist.

Its scarcity in modern times is thought to be due to mechanised farming. When hay was cut with scythes, it was cut later (and riper) and the corncrakes had time to nest and hatch off their chicks. Modern machinery annihilates them. There is no doubt that corncrakes were once common, even in the heart of the industrial Midlands.

One of my proudest possessions is a corncrake-caller, left to me in a will. The 'caller' consists of a wooden cogwheel, about the size of half a crown. It is mounted in a wooden fork that fits comfortably in the palm of the hand, and a flat wooden strip bears against the cogwheel which works against it on the principle of a football rattle – only far quieter.

Its owner told me that her uncles used it on the old Walsall racecourse. The 'musician' waited to hear a corncrake calling by the light of the full moon in the long grass on the edge of the racecourse. He then rotated the cog against the wooden spring, imitating the bird so skilfully that it thought it had a rival and emerged into the open to investigate, whereupon the other uncle shot it.

I gather they were good to eat and that all was grist that came to the mill in those hard times.

When their niece died, she bequeathed the caller to me, not because she thought I should execute corncrakes, but because she thought I was the only chap she knew who would appreciate it. She was quite right!

The corncrake season must have been about late May or early June. They are migratory birds and return at about the same time as the cuckoo. Pat Welsh was probably accurate in his prediction that there would be no warm weather until they arrived.

It is a depressing thought that these delightful birds have shrunk from commonplace to rarities in the last generation. There was a pair in a hayfield within three miles of my house about four years ago, but I have only heard them three times in my life and seen them once.

It set me wondering about the future of cuckoos. When I was a kid, cuckoos sang all day at this time of the year, even in Bloxwich where I was born. This year, I haven't heard a single call in the fields around the secluded woods I live near now. That doesn't mean they are universally scarce. I recently spent three days filming for a television programme in Wyre Forest in Worcestershire and they were never silent. But I have been around the country quite a lot since then, and my impression is that they are far less common than they were.

Our colleagues in the Common Market may be partly responsible. They net hundreds of thousands of migratory birds on their way to and from North Africa. And the French have just refused to stop shooting skylarks. This, combined with a disastrous drought, has had a devastating effect on many species.

Farmers and gardeners here may also be responsible because a lethal amount of poisonous sprays, designed to save crops from insect pests, wreaks havoc among the birds that feed on the insects. Whatever the cause, cuckoos are certainly less common in my area than they were. I hope and trust they will not follow the corncrake to extinction.

38. Conservation And The Credit Squeeze

I never thought I should see any good coming out of inflation but this is the Year of the Foxglove (1978), and there would be far less about in more prosperous times. One of the few economies squeezed out of the bureaucrats is that they mow the roadside verges less often than they did.

Miles of lush grass along every main road is obvious for all to see. It gives the illusion that somebody is bending over backwards to save a few hard-earned taxes. But it isn't only grass that lines the edges to our roads, it's wild flowers as well.

The lane up to our house has been a filmy mass of white cow parsley. Queen Anne's Lace it's called around here. And in places that enjoy a bit of shade, the purple foxgloves have been profuse. Perhaps their unaccustomed lushness is partly because there has been plenty of shade even where no trees grow, this wet and cloudy summer. Or it may simply be that many wild flowers are fonder of rain than most of us.

Whatever the cause, the feast of colour would not have been nearly so obvious if the flowers had not been allowed to grow long enough to bloom along roads where tens of thousands of motorists could enjoy them.

Conservationists were pleading for this long before the pounds had shrunk to pennies and Staffordshire, where I live, was notorious for its prissy-minded clerks in charge of the highways. Their one object in life seemed to be to produce verges as neat as city parks – where nothing grows that is not planted. A weed is simply a wild flower in the wrong place and the scientists have devised 'selective' weed killers that are devastating in their efficiency.

When I was a boy, it was a common sight at this time of year to see cornfields ablaze with poppies. If we see a field with poppies now, we label the farmer rudely as 'only dog-and-stick'. There are sprays for almost everything so that on efficient farms nothing grows in cornfields to compete with corn.

The damage to wild flowers doesn't stop there. You can't spray a field with weed killer without some of the spray drifting into the surrounding hedges. Indeed, you would probably want it to because it would be stupid to clear your land of weeds but allow it to be reinfested at once by seeds from the hedgerow surrounding it.

So, over the last few years, the wild flowers of the countryside have diminished alarmingly. It would obviously be unreasonable to expect farmers not to control weeds when such efficient ways are now available. Food is too essential to jeopardise it for the sake of aesthetic values, however attractive.

So the roadside verges really are one of our most important potential nature reserves. They cover tens of thousands of acres all over the country which cannot be used for any productive purpose. Ideally, they should be cut about once in every two years, always after the plants have had time to flower and seed and, quite as important, when the birds have finished nesting.

The purpose of this bi-annual cut is to prevent the verges degenerating into scrub woodland which would impede the view and smother the wild flowers. If land is left to 'nature', it first of all grows 'weeds' – or wild flowers, depending on your viewpoint. Then a dense scrub of hawthorn and ash and elder and willow replaces the flowers and, finally, what is known as 'climax' woodland of great forest trees grows through the scrub and smothers that.

So I do not advocate leaving the verges to nature, but managing them sensibly to get the best possible crop of beautiful truly wild, wild flowers. The fringe benefits will be that they will form the perfect haven for all sorts of wild birds to nest in peace, and for a rich tapestry of butterflies whose caterpillars feed on the flowers.

Surprisingly, wild birds and small animals do extremely well in spite of the traffic that roars by twenty-four hours a day. They are not afraid of mechanical noise nearly so much as they fear Man because generations of experience have taught them that no predator is as ruthless as we are. The men from the town hall do not take kindly to relinquishing their role of tidy-uppers.

But even they must admit the verges look prettier this year, the Year of the Foxglove, than they have done since mechanical cutters were all the rage. So let us enjoy the one good thing about the rise in prices by not spoiling the roadside beauty as soon as things pick up.

39. Sparrows Cock A Snook

Sam was a self-made man. He started in business as a coal heaver, working for somebody else, and the first rung in his ladder was when he bought a horse and cart. That was before the last war and, being a bit short of ready cash, he often had to ask for a down payment before he had enough to buy his customer's load at the pit head.

Hard work and enterprise enabled him to swap his horse and cart for a lorry – and then he forged ahead. By the end of the war, he had a haulage business which he cashed in, and retired when road transport was nationalised.

I watched his rise to prosperity because he used the same Black Country pub that I did. He was a large man, with a huge capacity for beer and an immense pot belly in which to store it, so he didn't have to waste his time going up the yard. He wore a blue serge suit, with a gold watch chain that could have owed its origin to a Cradley chain maker, the links were so large and impressive. That was at the pinnacle of his career. Every Hollywood script writer must have known him, too, because I have seen his double cast as a mini-tycoon in countless films.

After the war, petrol came off the ration – until some pompous little clerk, smelling redundancy if ration offices closed, put it back on coupons. Sam had more coupons that he could use for his business – and neither of us were much for pandering to bureaucratic whims, so he often helped me out. He once gave me a fistful to go on holiday and I innocently asked if he'd had his holiday yet. 'Holiday, my lad?' he said, 'holiday? It's all holiday for me. I ain't done no work for fifteen years – but I've done the hell of a lot of scheming!'

I was reminded of him last week by the most unlikely bird. A sparrow hawk. Now Sam had nothing obvious in common with sparrow hawks, which are slim and graceful birds, whose agile aerobatics are wondrous to watch. The only possible similarity was that our aristocratic ancestors placed them firmly at the bottom of the social scale so far as birds of prey went.

In the ancient sport of falconry, gyr falcons were reserved for kings and emperors, peregrines for noblemen, goshawks for yeomen and humble sparrow hawks for sporting parsons. And you can't get lower than that.

Not that Sam was a falconry fan. I doubt if he had ever heard of it. And come to think of it, it wasn't the sparrow hawk that reminded me of him so much as the sparrow hawk's prey – a bunch of house sparrows, as common as city gutter snipes.

At this time of year, when I am rearing ducklings and chickens and young pheasants, there is always a fair amount of chick crumbs and

A sparrow-hawk with his prey.

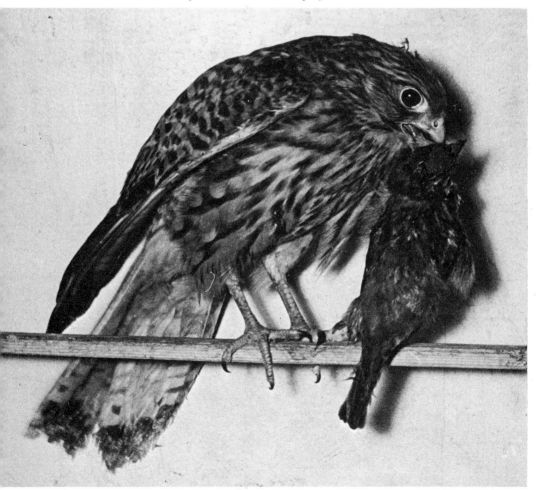

small grain that sparrows rate as five-star living. So they come out in flocks from the village to cash in on a heavily subsidised holiday in the country. We have often wondered why they choose a large berberis bush, on the edge of the lawn, for their lodging for no travel agent would recommend it. It has been clipped, over the years, to a spherical shape so that, from our window, it makes an attractive, brilliant green ball as boundary marker between the garden and paddock. The branches are dense and the wings covered in sharp thorns. It would be easy to suggest plenty of more comfortable roosting places.

Like Sam, our sparrows weigh up hard facts before arriving at their decisions. Having calculated the cons, they obviously decided that discomfort counted little when set against the most important pro of all from a small bird's point of view: safety.

During the winter, I put grain out in the paddock for the wild duck and pheasants. Flocks of small birds muscle in on this bounty, obviously under the impression I put it out for them. Several times a week, a sparrow hawk comes skimming along the edge of the wood, swoops over the grain and catches a bird before it realises what has hit it.

Most of the victims are yellowhammers or linnets because the sparrows are so cunning they keep a sharp enough look-out to dive for safety in time. At the first sign of danger, they retreat into the jungle of thorns at the heart of the berberis. Twice this week, we've had a ringside view of the hawk's frustration. She flies round the bush, but no sparrow is panicked into bolting for another refuge. She tries to follow them into the bush, but it is so dense that they can move around, but she can't. She glowers like a taxman on top, vainly trying to break their nerve.

They are so cocky they sit tight and swear at their tormentor. If their avian insults could be translated, they would frizzle up this page. Like Sam, they have done a hell of a lot of scheming. They too have made the grade themselves, and can cock a snook at anyone!

40. Campaign For Cleaner Milk

As from November 1979, Staffordshire became a county where brucellosis is eradicated by compulsion. Brucellosis is a particularly nasty complaint. The old name for it was contagious abortion, in cattle, which could be passed on to humans in the guise of undulant fever. This, as its name implies, is a high fever which attacks and subsides periodically. It is very difficult to cure and sometimes fatal.

When I was a kid, it was very common and nobody thought much about it. My father, who was a doctor, was fastidious about hygiene and always kept a couple of Jersey cows to provide the household with fresh milk, cream and butter. Although one cow would have provided more milk than we could drink, he kept two to cover the period when she was dry and giving no milk. In theory, this should have been for eight or ten weeks a year when she was dried off, and not milked, to allow her to get in top condition before she had her next calf. In practice, his cows were often more or less permanently dry because they aborted their calves and were hard to get in calf again.

Although I didn't know it then, this was undoubtedly because they had got contagious abortion. One of my regular chores, when I came home from work, was to borrow a cattle truck and take Daisy or Buttercup to the nearest pedigree Jersey bull. Nine times out of ten, the bull was unsuccessful but we continued to drink the fresh and untreated milk, eat butter-and-bread instead of bread-and-butter, and slurp oceans of cream over our strawberries. In theory, it should have tumbled us off our perches but we must have been tough. My father practised till he was seventy-eight and lived for years more in retirement. I still feel hale and hearty.

Undulant fever, or brucellosis, is still going strong. It is one of the occupational hazards of farmers and the veterinary profession. So the Minister of Agriculture has decreed that it shall be wiped out.

A scheme has been in force for years which offers the incentive of a higher price for milk and meat to farmers who maintain 'accredited' herds of cattle, free from the disease. The snag is that animals have to be tested periodically and any reactors are slaughtered. The disease is so terribly contagious that it is all too easy to get the herd reinfected from a neighbouring farm that is not accredited.

It can be passed between cows and bulls when they are mating, but the most dangerous time is when a cow calves normally or aborts. The whole area is then flooded with infection. This can strike any animals which pass that way or can be transmittted on the feet of animals or man.

The Ministry decided this would be less likely if whole areas were free, and the way to tackle the problem was to impose regulations county by county. Staffordshire dairy and beef farmers have now been included. Now their cattle will be tested regularly, whether they like it or not. Any reactors will be slaughtered and the farmers will receive only 75% of their value as compensation, and that only to a fixed maximum. Pedigree herds that do not pass could ruin their owners. Rigid regulations control if and where cattle can be moved and the standard of housing where they are kept. A breakdown in the health of the herd or even contact with a stray cow that is not accredited could sterilise movement for months and force sales in less profitable markets.

The man from the ministry orders that in-calf cows must be kept under observation and there are regulations about where they are to be kept and how to dispose of infected animals. Official advice suggests that 'visitors be kept to a minimum, that they should be made to wear overalls and special footwear because they can bring disease as well us carry it'. He omits to tell us how to do this with strangers using footpaths which may cross the land. It is a nettle that would cost too many votes to pluck!

There is no doubt that brucellosis is dangerous and unpleasant for man and beast and that, if there is a sensible chance of eradicating it, the trouble will have been well worth while. But the farmer does get the thick end of the stick for all our benefit. If his cattle get it through his bad husbandry, too bad. But if his cattle are put at risk by someone else's beast straying on to his land, or people walking across with the infection on their boots, my view is that he should be entitled to claim damages from them.

The farmer will have to put up with even more officials breathing down his neck. We shall share the benefits; we should also share the cost and inconvenience by restricting our movements in sensitive areas.

There is every chance that brucellosis will be brought under control by gradually extending the areas where infected cattle are compulsorily slaughtered. But in years to come when several generations of beasts have been bred which have never been subjected to the faintest whiff of infection, there is a real danger that natural resistance will also have been bred out. Cattle of the future may prove susceptible to the slightest chance of infection, as appears to be happening now with bovine T.B. in the West Country.

41. Harvest Hubbub

We live deep enough in the country for it to be pretty quiet at night. When I take the dogs out last thing, at this time of year, I don't usually hear much except the wind in the trees and a tawny owl hooting and wheezing to her newly-fledged chicks.

This year has been exceptional. The wet summer has produced a bumper harvest, but also a very damp one. In order to convert it from a pudgy mass to saleable grain that will bring in enough fivers to stuff the farmer's mattresses with sweet dreams, the surplus moisture has to be coaxed out.

Expensive grain driers have been designed to do just this. And they are noisy brutes! The one that forces its attentions on me is almost a mile away and there is a hill between us. So, in terms of sheer volume of sound, a factory inspector accustomed to the din of an iron foundry might have to wiggle a match in his ear to hear it.

But if he stood in the paddock with me, while the dogs are getting ready for bed, he would be the first to be aware of a high-pitched hum, as if his ears had seized with wax. It is a subtle, insidious sound that is easier to feel than hear, and it is hard to be definite about its direction. It is a sound that flatly refuses to go away, and when once it has been detected, it is impossible to ignore it.

I had a maiden aunt who was forever quietly humming hymn tunes just loud enough to be audible across the room – when once it had dawned what she was doing. It was impossible after this not to strain one's ears to try to decipher which tune she had chosen, a task I always found difficult, partly because I wasn't well up in such ditties and partly because she could never keep in tune.

Corn driers are rather like my aunt. They make just enough noise to be obtrusive without ever producing anything of interest. When they stop, the silence is golden.

Whenever I wake in the night, the faint hum is like holding a modern electronic watch to one's ear, and then, by breakfast time it dies away. Not because it has stopped: simply because other, louder sounds drown it out of consciousness.

When the weather is dry, combine harvesters snort and rumble across the fields, wolfing up corn and straw alike at a prodigious rate. The corn is threshed in the belly of the harvester and spurted from a spout into a trailer, dragged by a tractor. The straw is ejected in parallel ribbons that stretch across the field.

The sound of combines is something else everyone in the country almost fails to notice. Not because it is a quiet sound, but because the noise is so continuous it is possible to forget it is there.

I always look on it as a sign of prosperity; as a reward for a whole year's planning and effort by the farmer. It is the culmination of ploughing, harrowing, sowing the seed and controlling the weeds that wage continuous war on husbandry. So the combine's rumble has nothing in common with the sterile vocal do-gooding of my maiden

The old-fashioned method of stooking oats is rarely seen nowadays.

aunt. It is the virile basso profundo of successful males!

Not so the operation that comes after. When the corn is safely gathered in, it is the turn of the straw for harvesting. I am lucky enough to live in good dairying country, where cows are queens of all their masters' possessions. And cows need sweet dry straw to bed themselves down in winter.

So when the corn is gathered, the baler comes round to scoop up the golden straw and compress it into rectangular bales which are the precise size to be handled comfortably by a strong man and are geometrically efficient for building into ricks.

Although I respect straw balers for the job they do, they cause deep offence to anyone who has the instincts of an engineer. Instead of the smooth sophistication of high class machinery, they rattle and clank louder than a banger with its bearings seized. Every time the baler

Sadly, the modern devastation of straw by fire is now a common sight.

comes round the field, it sounds as if it will have fallen to pieces long before it has time to appear again. The wasp-in-the-ear signature tune of a corn drier is infinitely preferable.

But the harvest noise that really gets my goat is practically inaudible. It is the sinister hissing whimper of burning straw. The first warning that anything is amiss is the pall of black smoke on the skyline that might have been made by hordes of invading savages laying waste to a land that they have conquered.

'Waste' is the operative description. Work has become such a dirty, expensive word that, in arable parts, it has become cheaper to set fire to straw than harvest it. Fair fields are shrouded by smoke, as the straw below crackles and writhes in agony.

Mice and butterflies, spiders and small birds die by the billion because of our stupid disposable philosophy. Their death cries do not make much noise – but they give me many a sleepless night.

42. No Invitation Needed To This Feast

I sometimes wonder if our seasons have slipped. When I was young, October spelled toasted teacakes by the fire, and I was made to put on my muffler. In those days, the law of the survival of the fittest still operated in the Black Country and I was considered 'nesh' – or delicate – by the standards of the time.

So far this October, the neshest brat could have gone around without even a necktie on without catching his death of cold. The traditional 'little summer' we are supposed to enjoy in memory of St Luke has certainly been fact and not fiction.

Of course, when the clocks have altered, the nights really will start to draw in and unless there is a dramatic change in the weather, the light will look like winter and the air feel more like summer.

In the south last week, the leaves were falling and the mellow countryside was splashed with autumn tints. Our wood is predominantly oak and the leaves are still as green as Robin Hood's jerkin, though the acorns are only just beginning to fall.

There is a bumper crop this year and the deer have stopped grazing on the grassy rides and moved over among the trees. They wander haphazardly, but their apparent indecision is not so stupid as it looks. They stop every few yards to pick up an acorn because acorns to deer are as attractive as the most expensive chocolates to us.

For some time, there was no doubt that they benefited. Their coats were sleek and ripples of fat down their flanks were symbolic of their prosperity. By now, they should be rutting. Mid October is the season of mating for fallow deer, when the lusty bucks gather a large harem of does. Next June, the proof of their success will be the size and quality of fawns dropped in the summer bracken.

Our deer haven't even started the rut yet – they are still too busy looking for acorns that should be strewn in plenty. I thought, at first, that the temptation to feast was greater than the primitive urge to mate, but now I wonder.

Acorns are wonderful for fattening pigs and feeding deer – but they can be poisonous to cattle. Even deer can suffer from a surfeit. Perhaps the unusually wet summer produced great crops of wild fruits. Perhaps the deer will continue to search till they are gorged to the point where making love becomes more of a task than a pleasure?

The pheasants are behind-hand too. Most years, the acorns would have dropped by now and when supply does not meet demand, as happens most years, pheasants would be fat and sleek at the end of October but looking for alternative food supplies. Most years, there would still be grain to be gleaned in the stubbles but it has been uncommonly dry since harvest and the stubbles are ploughed and grown again on the most efficient farms.

So the pheasants are leaving the hedgerows and ploughland to compete with deer for acorns that are still out of reach in the trees. Sportsmen will not find them as easy to flush to their guns as when they are lying in turnips, next to the stubble.

Unfortunately, we have a crop we could well do without. Dead timber. The summers of 1976 and '77 were uncommonly dry and memories of forest fires and parched gardens are too vivid for comfort. What was less obvious was the effect on the trees. Silver birches are shallow-rooting trees and this time last year, most of ours seemed to have survived. Now, our over-optimism is obvious. All over the wood, birches two feet or so across the trunk have gone black in the leaf and are apparently dead.

For the next few weeks, the insensitive growl of my chain saw will shriek a lament to their memory as it brings them crashing down and dissects their trunks and branches into logs fit for our grates.

The lane to our house comes almost wide between low hedges with huge fields on either side. The first year here, we were well and truly snowed-up and could only reach the village, a mile away, by walking across the windswept fields. It taught me a lesson so that I programmed my work to be in my study writing from the middle of January to the end of February. I refused any engagements away from home during that time lest I could not get there or, worse, could not get back.

Then the council erected chestnut fences in the fields in an attempt to stop the snow in drifts before it reached the road, instead of blocking it. As it never really snowed hard again, we don't know if their plan would work and the danger has receded so far that I have quite a lot of work planned away from home in the New Year.

By the law of averages, we are about due for a hard winter to prove that unseasonable weather is only a freak.

43. Keeper Power

Gamekeepers and I have always had a love-hate relationship, because I am a relic from a generation of naturalists who were also interested in sport. We not only enjoyed studying wildlife, we were not above pitting our wits against the same creatures as quarry. We could see both sides of the argument.

My association with keepers started when I was about ten years old and a patient of my doctor-father gave me the run of his estate.

In those days, the head keeper on a great estate wielded enormous power. If he suspected that a farm labourer poached so much as a rabbit, he got the sack. If a tenant farmer complained too loudly about the damage pheasants were doing to his crops, his lease might not have been renewed.

So the idea of a small boy having leave to run free wherever he liked did not go down well with this particular head keeper. Small boys have sharp eyes and loose tongues so that no keepers' secrets are inviolate. Nevertheless, the squire was the boss so that the keeper decided that, since he couldn't beat him, he'd better join him.

He took me round his beat and taught me the elements of ferreting, snaring rabbits and trapping vermin. Most of the information with which he stuffed my head would not go down well with modern conservationists. His keeper's gibbet was decorated with carrion crows and hawks, stoats and owls, hedgehogs and jays and magpies.

Almost anything, it seemed, that didn't fall into the category of game was automatically classed as vermin. I learned that any bird with a hooked bill or any animal with canine teeth should be obliterated. His wife, who was very fond of cats, was compelled to keep hers on a chain by the hearth, as no cat was safe outside.

Knowing no better, I took all that he said as gospel truth. He was an honest man and genuinely believed what he said, so I had no cause to disbelieve him.

In those days, sportsmen-naturalists were very common. My basic love of natural history started by collecting butterflies and birds' eggs,

The barn owl feeds mainly on mice.

and my early association with keepers resulted in my growing up with a ferret permanently in my poacher's pocket. Such occupations are unfashionable now and frowned upon by conservationists.

They satisfy their collector's instinct by going bird watching and ticking off the species they see on a check list instead of shooting and stuffing them. They catch thousands of birds in mist nets and put numbered rings on their legs, getting proof of their prowess when someone else catches the same bird and reports the number of the ring on its leg, somewhere else. There is less difference between the two occupations than you may think (except from the bird's point of view!) because both pander to the collector's urge and the primitive hunting instinct.

As I grew up, I began to have doubts. I remember thinking a barn owl was the most beautiful bird I had ever seen and that no pheasant would justify the slaughter of such a creature. Later I learned that barn owls would prefer rats and mice to pheasants anyway, so that the question should never have arisen, though in the old-fashioned keeper's eyes, the hooked bill sealed the death warrant.

Badgers finally tipped the scale. I had a wonderful tame badger which lived with me for ten years,* and a succession of wild ones followed him. Several that lived in peace in our wood ended up being strangled in keepers' snares when they wandered on to the adjoining land.†

So far as I was concerned, it was war to the knife and I set about making the adjoining shoot uneconomic to run. A new keeper arrived at the beginning of this year and proved that it is never safe to generalise.

Badgers in any case are legally protected, but nothing much can be done if they are caught in 'mistake' for foxes. My new neighbour is not the type of keeper who makes such mistakes. He is one of the old school and, if he caught a badger, it would be a deliberate mistake.

It is never safe to generalise about any type of craftsman. I soon discovered that Tom is no enemy of badgers. He knows, as I do, that a badger snuffling about the floor of the wood will make the pheasants fly

---

* See *Badgers at my Window*, published in 1969.
† See *No Badgers in my Wood*, published in 1979.

up into the trees to roost. And when they are safe aloft, Charlie Fox can't catch them.

So he was happy enough to strike a bargain with me. He would not harm my badgers if I did not harbour foxes which play hell with my hens as well as with his game. It is a practical compromise which suits us both, and I find it encouraging to discover that there is good as well as bad, even in modern keepers, and that the friendships of my boyhood are not all seen through rose-tinted spectacles.

44. Death To The Deathwatch Beetles

Our bats have had a bad time this year. The wet summer provided fewer insects than normal, and the cold night rain never gave them much chance to get really active. Bats, bees and other insects have all had a pretty rough time.

There are about a dozen species of bat in this country, ranging from the common little pipistrelle, which looks like a flying mouse, to huge noctules with wing spans of over thirteen inches. Not many people notice these huge fellows because they fly very high, but they are the most superb aerial performers I have ever seen.

The time to watch them is at dusk on clear July nights competing with the swifts, or Jack-squealers as we called them in the Black Country. Swifts are larger than swallows and such marvellous fliers they even sleep and mate on the wing. Nothing you might think could compete with them in the air.

But noctules can. If you watch them through binoculars, high over-head on summer evenings, you will often see them competing with the swifts for insects that have floated high in the air on warm convection currents. The noctules are such brilliant performers, they can outfly the swifts and steal flies and moths from the tips of their beaks.

We get a few noctules in the wood and I often watch them but, so far as I know, not much can be done to encourage them to settle. They like hollows in trees. And they like to choose their own.

Pipistrelles or flittermice are not so prestigious but are easier to manipulate. When we came here, there were even fewer about than noctules, so I caught about thirty from a church lychgate and estab-lished them in my roofspace.

We had built a piece on to the house and made the eaves good so bats could not escape. I put my captive bats up there and shut them in with a plentiful supply of mealworms. Two days later, when the bats had had time to find comfortable roosting crevices in the rafters, we opened the exit slots around the eaves so they could creep out and fly in the world outside.

Experts on bats assured me the ones I caught and imprisoned would fly home like racing pigeons as soon as they got out. I have no means of knowing how right they were. All I know is that we have had a colony of bats – though not necessarily the same ones – in our roof ever since. Not only do they keep the roof free from woodworm and deathwatch beetles by catching the flying insects before they have time to lay their eggs, they also delight us with their acrobatics every summer night.

They are not, of course, as spectacular as the noctules because they are not as big and do not fly as high. But they whizz around at little more than head height, making timorous women guests squawk because they fear they will get caught in their hair. That is an old wives' tale. Bats are not so stupid and the only origin I can imagine for such

The pipistrelle bat in flight.

nonsense is that in less hygienic times, ladies' hair was not as free from insects as I hope it is today!

After a while, our colony of flittermice was joined by a smaller party of long-eared bats which, as their name implies, have huge rabbit-like ears to help locate their flying prey.

They should all be in hibernation by November, but the exceptionally mild autumn has encouraged them to stay airborne far later than usual. Normally, this would be a bad sign. When bats come out to hunt in winter, it often means they have not been able to put on enough fat on summer nights to last them through the difficult winter sleep. Later in the year, there are often few insects around for them to catch so they expend more energy hunting than they replace by eating the prey they catch.

This autumn may be slightly different because there have been moths fluttering against our windows right up until this last week. So perhaps the bats, which did badly during the wet summer, are making up for it now.

Even if they are, insects flying now should also be in hibernation, and there are few flowers to supply nectar to feed the moths. If the bats are having a field day now, it could well be at the expense of insects that should emerge in spring to lay the eggs for next year's crop. Killing the geese that lay the golden eggs!

The glorious autumn we have enjoyed so much and which we shall forget as soon as winter comes, could well have done tremendous damage to the insects that hibernate and the birds and animals which rely on them for food. Next year, perhaps, I shall have to look round for a vicar who doesn't like bats in his belfry to replenish the colony that are so welcome in my roof.

45. Sport For Working Dogs

The dogs have to behave themselves when I take them out into the wood. Temptation to chase deer or chop sitting pheasants never troubles them because I train them, from tiny puppies, that creatures I encourage on my reserve are not there for dogs to hunt.

There are exceptions though. Rats which take up residence in my grain store are on a loser if they think there is 'welcome' written on my mat. When I go out to feed the dogs last thing at night, they are happy to leave the warmth of the hearth, not only because they are sure of a plate of biscuits and succulent meat but because there is the chance of a little sport as well.

When I dismantled an old greenhouse years ago, I kept the cast iron heating pipes when I sold the rest for scrap. Each pipe is about four inches in diameter, and six or eight feet long and I have laid them carefully at strategic positions around the yard. When rats come out of the fields for food and warmth in autumn, they soon learn to pop into these pipes for refuge if they are caught out foraging in the open. Once they have 'gone to ground' in the cast iron pipe, they are safe from almost any enemy, or so they think.

So when I let them out at bedtime, the dogs rush round to see if a rat has taken cover in one of my carefully sited pipes. I know at once if one has because there will be a patient dog wagging her tail at each end of the pipe, willing me to come and do something about it.

When I have put the yard lights on and made the dogs sit back far enough to allow the rat to get clear of his refuge, it is a simple matter to poke something up the pipe to encourage him to move. Although a job for working dogs, they certainly regard it as sport so it is a reward for their forbearance in not molesting deer and other creatures I wish to preserve.

I suppose in the course of a year they kill sixty or seventy rats about the yard and buildings. Without their help, we could have a plague of the wretches, but I make no pretence that I do not enjoy the sport as much as the dogs do.

For more than twenty years, while I worked in industry, my hobby on Sunday mornings was to take a bag of ferrets and some good terriers to go ratting by invitation of my farmer friends. No quarry is quicker at making split-second decisions about how to escape from the tightest corner. Most men who are that cool under pressure end up as tycoons or top politicians.

Because I manage my wood as a reserve for species under pressure, I try to keep the number of their enemies within bounds. Too many carrion crows, magpies, grey squirrels, stoats or foxes would make life impossible for ground nesting birds, song birds, or even larger birds like herons.

So if the dogs chase a squirrel they find feeding on the ground, I do nothing to discourage them. Friends who call here often wonder how the dogs know what is allowed and what is forbidden. The answer is simple. I never take on a new dog after it is eight weeks old, so any bad habits it develops can be blamed on no one but myself. I always take it out to feed the poultry as a tiny pup, while I can still run faster than it can! Then I can head it off or chuck a handful of corn at it to distract it the moment it makes a wrong move.

So it grows up to believe it is not allowed to chase anything at all, at which stage I take it among cattle and sheep to drive the lesson home. When it is past the puppy stage, and sensible, it begins to come out with the older dogs at night, to see if there are any rats about. Then, very gradually, it is allowed to enlarge its scope to include grey squirrels and other animals I wish to keep in check.

All working dogs have a natural hunting instinct. Belle, my Alsatian, came from an illustrious line of police dogs and her relatives have been trained to regard criminals as quarry. Not having many criminals on my visiting list – so far as I know! – I have encouraged her to treat my friends as honoured guests. But she's nuts on rats.

During the recent snow, our paddock was spattered by a rash of molehills. I was surveying them, lost in admiration for any creature which could tunnel through the frozen ground and heave up mounds of soil through the iron-hard crust. Belle was troubled by no such senti-mental nonsense. Her delicate nose sensed a mole somewhere near the surface, so she started to dig, presumably in the belief that if a mole could dig up to the surface, she could dig down to the mole.

I knew the ground was so sodden the mole could not dig very deep before he came to the water level and would drown, so I called Belle to heel on the grounds that the contest would be unsporting.

My wife, a keen gardener who hates moles, agrees with Belle that I should let my working dogs work!

46.   A Ferret On My Finger

December is the traditional month when countrymen in my young days went rabbiting. It was a good method of working off a hangover, because the air was always sharp and invigorating (at least, on Christmas cards). The exercise of digging tons of soil to find a ferret that had chosen to stay below ground to eat his victim, was guaranteed to restore a flagging appetite.

Ferreting was the key because ferrets are such unpredictable brutes that it was impossible to forecast whether their behaviour would be impeccable or whether they would lie-up or get lost.

So for most of my life I have taken the precaution of keeping a ferret myself so that, if it worked well, I scooped the praise and if it misbehaved, I had no one but myself to blame for not training it better.

For the last two years I have been ferretless, and Belle, my Alsatian bitch, is the first dog of my life which is not broken to the ferret. By that I mean she is not trained to differentiate between a ferret and, say, a rat or rabbit or other legitimate quarry. I am perfectly aware that if she found a stray ferret in the wood, there is every chance that she would catch it and bring the trophy to me. Dead.

Counting this a sad reflection on me as a dog-man, I borrowed a ferret from Tom Brown, our local keeper, to remedy my defect. I planned to keep it for about a week, train Belle not to harm it, and then return it before I was due to be working away from home for the night.

I had another reason for wanting to borrow a ferret which was quite unconnected with a ferret's normal job of ratting or rabbiting. I reared a few guineafowl this year and they are normally noisy birds which have a loud insistent alarm call when anything disturbs them, and a monotonous cry of 'come-back, come-back, come-back' which seems to continue from dawn to dusk when nothing exciting is happening.

For some reason that I haven't discovered, my guineafowl are exceptionally silent this year and I particularly wanted to get a tape recording of their voices for a radio programme I was doing. The last twice that the producer had called, we had taken a tape recorder out but the birds had refused to utter a note. They had dried-up at the sight of the microphones as stupidly as the dumbest of dumb blondes.

Ferrets, I thought, that'll stir them into action! I'll borrow Tom's ferret, make the guineafowl sing and train Belle not to touch it while I've got it around.

It was a perfectly practical thing to try because they yell their heads off at the sight of a stray dog, let alone a fox or stoat. All I needed to do was to put a little collar on the ferret, tether it out in the open on a few yards of line and wait for the guineafowl to see it. All hell would be let loose.

Tom brought the ferret round before the producer arrived and said, 'Mind how you catch hold of her. She's a bit sharp.' He was teaching

A ferret is set to work.

his grandmother to suck eggs. Few keepers bother to handle ferrets as much as they should, so that it's always wise to treat keepers' strange ferrets with due respect. I've done it all before.

I left the ferret in her carrying box till the producer came and got her out to show him. Tom's ferret was a little beauty. Having handled ferrets all my life, I clenched my fist to stretch the skin tight over the back of my hand and proffered it to her to smell.

Ferrets are not fierce by nature; they are shy creatures. If they bite you, it is usually in self-defence, for when they are bold and confident, they are tame and affectionate. Tom's ferret smelled my outstretched hand and was satisfied. If she had tried to bite it, the skin was too taut for her to get a grip and her teeth would have slipped off harmlessly.

I explained the technique to the producer, who was visibly impressed. Picking the ferret up, I was pleased to see how relaxed she was in my hands, how comfortably she lay in my warm but gentle grip.

Forgetting all about her as we talked, my other hand came within her reach. The skin wasn't taut and I hadn't had the manners to allow her to sniff it for reassurance. She laid hold of my forefinger, holding it between her four needle-sharp canine teeth as firmly as if it were in a vice.

When things go slightly wrong, my language tends to get a little flowery, but this time I didn't say a word. This really is a sign that things have gone badly wrong. I was concentrating so hard on choking her off that deathly silence was the order of the day.

The guineafowl saw us and raised hell all right, though whether in fear or mirth I never discovered. I returned the ferret to Tom with my thanks. Belle is still waiting to be trained.

47.   Sweet Dreams

My father, who was a Black Country doctor, used to say more of his patients died of eating too much than of drinking too much. In his day, it was quite a compliment to say, 'What a man! He *can* chop!' And the old saying, 'The goose is a foolish bird. Too big for one, not enough for two', confirmed the theory.

I stretched out before our log fire after dinner on Christmas Day, drowsily recalling such good old days, while I topped off my meal with a third glass of home-made sloe gin. Old-timers had no monopoly of intemperance, I thought, but it did raise my doubts about my own expectation of life. I really must slim now the holiday is over!

Then I noticed that, if I was drowsy, the dogs were clapped out. Nothing makes a hearth more homely than a comfortable dog stretched out in luxury on the rug. All three of ours were telling the world with eloquent grunts and snores that they, too, had dined well if not wisely.

I noticed that Tick, my German pointer, was twitching in her sleep. The muscles in her legs flickered so I wondered if her subconscious mind was urging her to get cracking and catch whatever was exciting her. Her ears twitched and she raised her lips to show her formidable fangs but the whole fearsome display subsided into a charade when, instead of growling or snarling, she gave the show away by uttering puny little squeaks.

'Dreaming,' I thought. 'I wonder what she's catching?' And then I thought again.

I thought of the scientists who would laugh such fancies to scorn, claiming animals act by instinct and not by intelligence. They would write off my theories about dreams by claiming animals could imagine nothing they could not actually see.

Tick got even more enthusiastic, squeaking and even rolling her eyes without regaining consciousness. If she was not dreaming, vividly as we do, I will eat my cap.

There is no doubt in my mind that animals do dream. Anyone who has had a favourite dog must have watched it reliving its triumphs and disasters as often as he has dreams or nightmares himself. And if animals can dream, they are capable of imagining things far more vividly than arrogant boffins imagine. Nor does it need the stimulus of good food and the comfort of a fire to trigger off their minds.

I believe dogs and probably other animals are sensitive enough to react to thought waves as intangible as telepathy. Over the past few years, I have been involved with a number of sheep dog trials. I have marvelled at the skills of shepherds who can train their dogs to round up stubborn sheep and guide them through the intricacies of a course laid out to test both man and dog.

With one whistle, the shepherd can send his dog off into the distance, far past the bunch of sheep he wants collecting from some craggy fell. The next whistle will drop the dog in his tracks, as if he had been shot, and he will stay there, quivering with excitement till he hears whether his master wants him to go right or left.

Then he will bring the sheep fast, or slow, as the distant whistle commands, right up towards his master. But the hardest job of all is to persuade the dog to drive the sheep away again. His instinct is to retrieve things, as a puppy will chase and fetch a ball.

The scientists will say there is nothing miraculous about driving away again; that it is just a matter of training. So it may be, for ordinary work on the farm. But in a competitive sheep dog trial, there is often much at stake. The dog may understand nothing about prestige of championships or that the stud fees of champions rocket, but his master does.

The men get as tense as actors on the stage and, when they get an unusually stubborn bunch of sheep, even stolid countrymen get a flutter of butterflies in their tummies. That is the time to watch the dog. No word need be spoken, no perceptible inflection of command, but the dog will sense his master's frazzled nerves and go to pieces too. Time after time I have seen trials lost, not because of any fault of the dog but simply because the shepherd's nerves have cracked under the strain and infected the dog with the jitters too.

That could be a form of telepathy, a subtle communion of minds, far more sophisticated than dreams before a comfortable fire. I do not even think it is an uncommon state of canine mind, for I observe the same thing daily, not only between man and dog but also between one dog and another.

When Tick finds something interesting in the wood, her excitement immediately communicates to the other dogs, even when they are yards away, out of sight behind a bush. With no sight or sound I can detect, they rush to see what is afoot. The unexplained mysteries of animal minds are far deeper than the brightest boffins dream about.

48. The Good Life In The Dog-House

Lucky dogs at a Birmingham dogs' home are promised turkey and chocolate drops for Christmas and the RSPCA is seeking good homes for enough beagles to start a pack of hounds.

The beagles are luckier than the strays because some of these were destined for medical research. If the beagles had not been rescued, they might have ended their days in experiments for germ warfare or inhaling tobacco fumes to test the relationship of lung cancer and smoking. You don't need a vivid imagination to picture the agony stinking tobacco would be for a nose as sensitive as a hunting dog's.

So it is not surprising tha such snippets of news send all sorts of do-gooders into emotional tizzies. Dog lovers detest the thought of dogs being used in any kind of medical research. They get far more excited by threats to their furry riends than by catastrophes to human cousins in far-off places.

It is one thing to try out new techniques on animals if the knowledge gained can relieve genuine human suffering. The use of animals to test out new cosmetics is quite another matter. I would not hazard a hair of my dogs' heads simply to develop a beauty aid to bolster up the sagging charms of women who wish to pass themselves off as lamb when they are long past mutton. And anyone stupid enough to ruin his health by smoking deserves all he gets without ruining the health of innocent dogs as well. I certainly wouldn't condemn a beagle to gasp its life away in a nicotine mask to protect such fools from their folly.

Fond as I am of dogs, I shall not be at the head of the queue for beagles, though. I do not believe that any dog that has been selectively bred for generations to hunt in a pack is likely to be blessed with a high IQ.

I once watched a pack of hounds hunting a fox in woodland. When one hound got a whiff of the scent, he began to 'speak' to the line, or bay his song of hate. Every other hound in the pack converged on him to share the intoxicating scent. When they got a whiff, they all screamed with delight and the woodland echoed with their cry.

As soon as he heard the rumpus, the fox slipped quietly out at the far end of the wood and left them to it. A hound which could think for himself would have forestalled this by sneaking on ahead and waiting for his mates to send the quarry on. If he had succeeded, he would have caught the fox and there wouldn't have been a hunt. So the huntsman would have destroyed him for having too much initiative.

Pack dogs are like that. They are selectively bred not to think. I prefer dogs bred for intelligence as sheep dogs are, so anyone who finds a home for the rescued beagles is more charitable than I am.

The strays in the dogs' home might be more in my line. Dogs which just 'happen' through chance alliance at least have the virtue of not being selectively bred for looks at the expense of brains and stamina. Some of the happiest days of my childhood were shared with Mick, a mongrel bull terrier which more than made up in brain any deficiency in conventional good looks.

When I get a new dog, I always pick a pup young enough for me to train myself. It is so much easier to nip incipient faults in the bud than to cure them when they have had time to develop.

The saddest sight of all, to my eyes, is an intelligent dog which someone has bought for a pet for some spoiled, unruly kid. Good-humoured dogs will put up with all sorts of nonsense from unintelligent masters. They will suffer teasing with dignity and mauling about with considerable patience. The thing which breaks their hearts is the sudden discovery that they are neglected and unwanted despite their loyalty.

That is how most strays land-up in dogs' homes. They are bought as presents for undisciplined brats by unimaginative relatives. They are pampered and petted for a few weeks, until the novelty wears off. Then they are discarded with no more thought than if they were broken toys, although they have given their hearts to their masters. They are turned out on to the streets to fend for themselves – and there is soon disruptive work for idle paws to do.

They get unpopular with neighbours, and the best that lies in store for them is that some kind soul picks them up and takes them to the dogs' home. Their misery may be less spectacular than the indignities of the vivisection laboratory but neither is necessary.

So I wish the beagles well and I hope that the strays will find a better home next time. I don't grudge any of them a scrap of turkey or a crumb of chocolate this Christmas.

49.   Winter Wonderland

There is no silence, in a wood, like the silence when dry and powdery snow lies on the ground. It muffles every footfall so that grown and clumsy men drift through the trees as stealthily as their shadows. Birds, which have nothing to sing about in such weather, sit with feathers fluffed out to conserve their body heat more efficiently than an eider-down.

The clatter as a wood pigeon flies up when he sees wha he probably mistakes for a human ghost, is as loud in contrast as a lorry disgorging a ton of bricks. Last weekend was different. The snw had come all right, but it was not dry and powdery. A gooey blanket, about a foot thick,

The frozen pool at Goat Lodge.

was so wet that it congealed beneath every footfall into ice.

I often think how lucky I am to have chosen a job where I work from home with no boss but myself. I have been so busy this autumn that the current book I am writing has got shoved aside to make way for more urgent work until it is several weeks behind schedule.

Before I can get down to serious writing, the animals have to be watered and fed. Whatever the weather. This is not much of a problem when the snow is dry and powdery, because it is only the work of a moment to scoop it aside and provide a dry bed to scatter the corn.

When I went out last Sunday morning, I could not open a single gate out of the yard. When I forced them a foot or so ajar, the snow behind congealed into hard ice and jammed the whole thing solid. I had to climb through the sitting-room window, which took me to the other side of the yard gates, and take a shovel to clear the snow behind the gates before I could start to feed at all.

Walking up the wood with a bucket of corn to feed the pheasants got me glowing with exhilaration and I stopped to admire the trees which had been coated with virgin snow. There was nothing silent about the wood now, though. Every few minutes there was a crack as sharp as a whiplash. I thought at first it was an intruder with a rifle and was surprised that Belle, the Alsatian, took no notice. She never misses an invitation to see off uninvited guests which she regards as her brand of quarry.

She was wiser than I was, for the sound was not man-made. Every shattering crack was a branch weighed down by its burden of wet snow. It sorted out the weak and rotten first, leaving them to lie unlamented on the woodland floor where insects would invade them and birds would eat the insects.

But it was not only the rotten trees that suffered. The whole crown came out of an oak tree, fifty or sixty feet high. When I went to examine it to see if it was rotten in the heart, it was as sound as a bell. The weight of snow and the driving wind had shattered it into splinters as jagged as if it had been hit by lightning.

Hawthorn trees seemed to be the worst sufferers and one about twenty feet high and six inches across had fallen across the drive and brought down my neighbour's telephone wire. So the first job was to saw that up into pieces small enough for me to lug away before someone piled into my boundary fence trying to avoid it.

By that time, I was warmer than plenty of clerks sitting in centrally heated offices so I got out the old tractor to do a bit of snow clearing. I have made a Heath Robinson arrangement of an oak plank bolted to the back of the tractor so that it can be raised and lowered hydraulically. By dropping it on the ground and skating off in reverse at high speed, a huge wedge of snow is pushed backwards clearing the yard and entrance to the drive in about a quarter of an hour. It is a fiendishly cold job, done in cold blood, but an exhilarating experience after enough hard work to get the steam up.

Not all wildlife suffer as badly as you might think. Mice and voles are all right because they tunnel under the snow where their normal food is buried and, since they are out of sight of hawks and owls, their chances of survival dwindle very little. Badgers grow lethargic and lie in their snug setts shamelessly and foxes get a few easy meals by catching almost anything which the cold overcomes.

But I watched a party of fallow deer actually cashing in on their misfortune. The grass was so deeply covered that they had to scratch through the snow to win every mouthful. But deer are tremendous browsers on trees. Although few leaves are showing, except honeysuckle, the sap is beginning to flow and buds are forming beneath the unappetising bark. They had already eaten what they could reach, but the weight of wet snow humbled many whippy saplings and made them bow towards the ground. The deer were wandering through the wood, nipping off the tasty buds as if some unseen hand were proffering them.

By the time I had done my chores, wandered through the wood and had my lunch, it was almost time to start to feed again. So the book is yet another day behind schedule.

50. Our Badger Dines Late

Last Sunday will remain in my memory as a real Red Letter Day for the rest of my life. At 1 a.m. precisely, a wild badger pushed open the wooden swinging gate – my 'badger gate' – into a small wire netted coop and helped himself, or herself, to the dish of flaked maize and golden syrup I had put there for such visitors.

I am certain about the exact time he arrived although I was fast asleep. He clocked in when he came and left the evidence on a graph in my study which 'punches up' the hour and minute when the swinging badger gate is entered.

It is an old contraption, dreamed up by a friend from the days when I used to work in a factory. He converted a scrap temperature recorder to give me a permanent record of the activities of Bill Brock, my hand-reared badger who lived in an artificial sett near the house but who was free to wander the woods outside.*

'Experts' on badger behaviour will tell you just when you ought to go badger watching. They claim to be able to foretell the exact time they will emerge and start feeding in the open, and when they will return to their sett to sleep the day away.

I kept records of times my badgers came and went every night for five consecutive years. I think, but I'm not sure, that they got up early if they had had difficulty in finding enough food the night before and had gone to bed hungry. But if they had had a right good blow-out, it was not uncommon for them to have a lie-in next night! The only certain thing about their activities was that they were quite unpredictable. Whatever the experts say about their coming out half an hour after sunset, or going to bed at dawn, my badgers hadn't heard of their timetable! So I didn't take much notice of the boffins, but accumulated a mass of information for myself. It may not have been of world-shattering importance, but I enjoyed watching the badgers I had reared enjoying themselves.

One of the snags about such work is that the scientists say, with some justification, that it is unreliable. They say it is never safe to assume

* See *Badgers at my Window*.

that the actions of hand-reared animals are typical of what their wild relations would do.

So when my badgers died, I determined to spike the guns of my critics by repeating the work with genuinely wild badgers that lived in and around my wood. I made some attractive sites for them to dig their own setts, by bulldozing piles of roots together and covering them with earth. The roots provide dry shelter which they know instinctively is almost impregnable. The soil is soon covered with grass and weeds and the grass roots supply a warm and waterproof roof so that they regard the whole site as an eminently desirable plot for a high-class badger residence.

It all worked like a dream and this time four years ago, there was a wild sow badger with cubs in a sett she had dug herself within sight of

A snared sow badger showing deep cuts under her right arm pit and round the neck. The swollen teats indicate that she had recently cubbed.

my study window. Then the dream turned into a nightmare. I discovered a dead badger in a snare within half a mile of home. She was a nursing mother and the wire had caught her round the body and bitten into her udder, slicing it open.

Furious about this badger and worried about 'my' sow and cubs at home, I fetched the police. Badgers are protected by law and I was after the blood of whoever had set the snare. The police were powerless because, although it is illegal to kill badgers deliberately, the man who set the snare claimed he had set it for a fox and killed the badger accidentally. And it is not illegal to snare foxes on ground you own or control.

I was never able to establish the cause, but all the badgers in my wood subsequently disappeared as there was no way I could stop them straying into danger over my boundaries. For three years, there were no badgers in my wood.*

Now there is a keeper next door who is interested in my work and, far more important, holds no grudge against badgers.

Last autumn I noticed freshly excavated earth outside the sett near the house and I knew that the first badger had returned and he, or she, has been there, on and off, ever since. I have been so careful not to disturb it for fear of driving it away, that I haven't yet caught a glimpse to give me a clue whether it is a boar or a sow.

But I have been putting out a bowl of flaked maize soaked in syrup each night because badgers have as sweet a tooth as I have. To stop the deer or duck or pheasants getting there first, I put the bowl in a wire-netted chicken coop, fitted with the swinging badger gate which a badger can easily push open from either side. I fixed the gate open until he was feeding freely.

He missed the first night after I let it swing-to but greed soon overcame caution and he continued to feed after that. Then I fitted the little switch, like they had on old-fashioned sweet shop doors, and wired it up to the graph in my study.

Last Sunday, he dined at 1 a.m. and he has been about the same time each morning since then. When the nights draw out, I hope he will come earlier so I can start badger watching again where I left off when my other badgers disappeared.

* See *No Badgers in my Wood.*

51.   Save Our Oaks

The long winter and truant spring have made the primroses and wild daffodils more welcome than ever. Our wood was sombre and lifeless well into May but, almost overnight it seemed, we had skipped spring and arrived in early summer.

Last week, going down the M5 to Bristol, the countryside would never have looked more beautiful if it had not been spattered with monumental dead elms. Leafy Warwickshire and the Cotswolds owed so much of their attraction to the wonderful elm trees that thrived in every hedgerow, the devastation caused by Dutch elm disease means they now stare with lifeless eyes whichever way you look.

The stupidity is that our status as an island should have protected us from the plague. The virus which spread the disease would not have arrived here if we had not imported it with timber from abroad. Once here, it was spread by elm bark beetles which were contaminated by the virus and passed it on to sound trees.

Experts played down the danger, claiming that the first hard winter would halt the attack, but all who travel around the country can see how wrong they were. Even the optimists have written off our native elms as a dead loss, though perhaps, one day in the future, a few immune suckers may sprout and delight future generations with sound trees. But not, I fear, in our time.

The one good thing that may have come out of our defeat by the disease is that it has detonated some of the scientists out of their cosy cloud-cuckoo land. Faced by the catastrophe of millions of trees they could neither save nor replace, they turned their attention to other species that have not yet come under attack.

They realised that oak wilt is raging in North America and that if it arrived on our shores it could affect our oaks. Elms were predominantly hedgerow trees so that, although they may be very conspicuous to visitors to the countryside, they are less commonly grown by the hundred as woodland trees. Nothing is more English than an English oak and the possibility of whole tracts of woodland being devastated would be appalling.

Oak wilt is a fungus disease, not unlike Dutch elm disease, since the fungus enters the trees either through the roots or through being spread by insects, causing wilting, discolouration and death. It can also be spread by birds and squirrels.

Fortunately, it is far more lethal to the American Red Oaks than to the white variety which is native to our shores. But foresters have developed the habit of surrounding their ugly conifer plantations with a few rows of red oaks. These grow far more rapidly than English oaks and have leaves which turn a brilliant red in autumn, acting as a gaudy screen to camouflage the sterility of foreign firs. It would be no bad thing to forgo the attractions of these red oaks lest they act as carriers if oak wilt should ever come. The sensible plan would seem to be to place a total ban on the import of oak timber from any country where there is danger from the disease – but it is not as easy as that.

American oak is largely used for whisky vats – we export around six hundred million pounds worth of whisky a year, as well as what we sink ourselves. And money talks. American oak is also widely used in trade, especially for making furniture, so that the commercial opposition to banning its import, whatever the risk to our native trees, would be formidable.

So an Act was passed, under the title Importation of Wood and Bark (Prohibition) (Great Britain) Order 1977, laying down conditions which the optimists hope will prevent oak wilt following Dutch elm disease as the number one despoiler of our countryside. It specifies that all oak wood imported in the round must have had the bark removed before shipment and the wood must have been dried out to a maximum of twenty per cent moisture or fumigated under supervision.

Modern society is growing more and more violently opposed to serious threats to our environment. And so it should. The example of devastation of millions of English elms simply because of laxity in allowing diseased timber to be imported has left its mark. If enough people growl at the politicians, we may still get laws with enough teeth, not only to avoid the introduction of oak wilt, but diseases affecting farm livestock and poultry, and the greatest threat of all, which is that of rabies which could arrive on some smuggled pet.

52.   The Biter Bit

A woman telephoned to know if I thought she'd seen an otter; she wouldn't give her name and was evasive about the location. All she would say was that she 'saw it in a ditch'.

One of the hazards of my occupation as a naturalist is that strangers frequently write or telephone with the most bizarre requests. Anything from wanting to know how to create a nature reserve in a corner of the garden, to how to stop rabbits eating the roses.

I wasn't particularly interested whether the present enquirer had seen the Loch Ness monster or a man from outer space, so I told her to be more specific or to stop wasting my time.

'Before I do that,' she said, 'what is your attitude to otters?' Most of the people who would bother to seek my opinion already know that I am totally convinced that otters are an endangered species, and would do all in my power to protect them, even from walkers. (See Nos. 00, 00 and 00.)

Reassured, she confided that she had seen her otter in a part of north Staffordshire I know fairly well – where there is no sizeable river. I was mildly surprised.

How did she come to see it? I asked. She said that she was out walking with her dogs and, seeing a movement in a ditch, she 'set them on'.

Was she a farmer? I asked. It turned out that she was just taking the dogs for a walk and thought it was a bird, or she wouldn't have set the dogs on. In my view, people who go for walks over other people's property and encourage their dogs to hunt without permission, deserve to get them shot; so I told her, in words she could well understand, what would happen to her dogs if I ever found them on my land.

We were not getting on too well and I should have hung up if the mysterious animal had seemed to be anything else. But otters are getting so scarce that I like to know where as many are as possible so that I can do anything I can to ensure that they are not disturbed.

In this case, I am certain it was not an otter. The woman's labrador retriever had emerged with the creature 'hanging on his lip'. An otter, weighing 20 lbs. or so, would do far more damage than that.

The dog's owner had seen 'quite a bit of white' on it, so I suggested it might have been a stoat, which she thought was 'one of those animals with white on their tails'.

'That's it,' I said, 'only it's black. That's the tippet of ermine on the mayor's cloak, you know.'

'What about coypu?' she asked. Coypu are like giant water rats which have escaped from fur farms near the Norfolk Broads where they used to provide nutria fur, and they have colonised parts of East Anglia where rat catchers from the Ministry of Agriculture have been fighting a losing battle with them for years.

We wrote them off, partly because she could not have mistaken one for anything else if she saw it hanging on the lip of her dog. Nor would

Coypu are like large water rats.

the dog forget the experience! It is as big as a fair-sized fox terrier.

I suppose it could have been a common rat. A big one, but my inquisitor would have none of that. I was insulting her dog if I thought he couldn't kill a rat.

And then it occurre to me that it might have been an escaped mink. Mink have been escaping from fur farms for many years and often settle down and survive quite well in the wild. Too well for comfort.

In life, mink are as predatory and slinky as the blondes they adorn in death. They are like large ferrets, but far fiercer and more agile and once they escape from the mink ranch, they are difficult to recapture. They have colonised whole areas of river bank in Devon and a great many isolated places all over the country. Rivers each side of the Pennines from Derbyshire northwards are troubled by these pests.

I had heard isolated stories about creatures which might be mink in Staffordshire, but have never been able to confirm them. Nor do I want to because they are a dreadful scourge. They can kill small birds and even quarry as large as ducks and geese. They are far worse than foxes for domestic poultry because they are sinuous enough to squeeze through the wire netting of hen pens. Shutting the hens in for the night won't protect them from the mink, unless the hens are actually in enclosed houses.

The mink love water and can also catch fish. Some people even say that they compete directly with otters and might slaughter otter cubs while the bitch otter is away hunting for their food. I have never seen proof of this but it would be by far the worst of their crimes if it were so.

So perhaps the woman who telephoned me had been hunting mink and not otter. If she meets it again, I hope she'll take a decent dog with her which won't let go if it nips him on the lip!

53. Odds Against Survival

Two mornings running, soon after it was light, I noticed a rabbit on the bulb patch by the gate into the yard. There are a lot of rabbits this year, and I shouldn't have given my discovery a second thought if I hadn't been curious to know what it was eating. I couldn't see anything attractive to rabbits for yards around.

Going over to see if there was any freshly nibbled herbage, I soon found why she had been there. There was a slight bulge in the surface of the soil, as if a mole had raised the top layer of soil instead of having to excavate it as a molehill. This tunnel had not been dug by any mole. It was a blind passage, about four feet long, ending in a chamber about as big as a pudding basin.

The reason that neither my wife nor I had spotted it before was that, when the rabbit I had seen had left it, she had carefully filled in the entrance.

Rabbits often build such 'blind' tunnels or 'stops' so that they can have their young away from the colony in the rabbit warren. They are spiteful creatures and the bucks are not above savaging and sometimes eating their own young.

So this doe had found a quiet spot, dug her stop, had her kittens and I had only noticed her by chance, when she had called to suckle them. When they had gorged on her milk, she stopped up the end of the hole so that nothing else would find them (except perhaps a fox or badger!) and she only visits them as often as is necessary to feed them.

The expression 'breeds like rabbits' is no flight of fancy. In theory, a doe rabbit is able to produce a litter of four or five about once a month. Her gestation period is twenty-eight eays and she is ready to mate again within two days of having her young, all through the breeding season which lasts about eight or nine months of the year. Even this depends on the weather and, if it is mild and there is sufficient food available, rabbits have been seen to breed in every month of the year.

But the capacity to reproduce is far more sophisticated than this. The doe remains attractive to the buck while she is on heat but she does not submit to mating until the last few hours of her attractiveness, when the urge is at its peak and there is maximum chance of success.

But the most important mechanism in rabbits' armoury for survival is the power to reabsorb their own embryos. Half way through her term, if things are not going as well as they might, the doe can reabsorb her own embryos, come into heat within a few hours and start again, instead of wasting valuable time bearing and rearing a smaller litter than prevailing conditions might support. (See also No. 32.)

This phenomenon can be triggered off by a number of outside factors, including bad weather, but available food supply is the most common. When crops fail, it is obvious that the doe rabbit feels the effect first.

At about her 12th to 14th day, when her babies are about as big as walnuts inside her, she doesn't abort them. They are simply reabsorbed into her system. By the next time she has conceived, conditions might have improved.

Looking at a colony of rabbits, playing and eating and breeding at the edge of a wood, it is easy to imagine them as a model for democratic equality. But no animals have a more rigid pecking order. There are boss-bucks and women's-libber does – who even boss the boss-bucks.

This is even obvious in their overwhelming urge for reproduction. At the first signs of hard times, it is not the boss does who reabsorb their young but the poor little souls at the bottom of the pecking order. This leaves what food there is for the dominant matrons most likely to produce the rabbits of the future. They fight for the best breeding quarters, drive weaklings away from the best patches of food and are most attractive to the huskiest bucks.

It is really a form of birth control in reverse. Instead of the members of society with most advantages having the smallest families, as often happens in human society, rabbits with the best chances of survival have most young. Over-population is really another way of saying that there are too many mouths for the available food to fill.

Rabbits have a marvellous mechanism for increasing their numbers to match the food supply in good times – but Nature cuts down their numbers when times are hard.

Mankind has no monopoly of wisdom!

54. The Fate Of The Odd Man Out

The Canada goose which nested on the island has hatched out. She had had a pretty traumatic time. For one thing, there had been great competition for the most desirable building site, and since geese do not deal in cash, they had settled the matter by the primitive doctrine that Might is Right.

Since, at the peak of the nesting season, there had been no less than five pairs of beady little eyes coveting the one small island that is safe from foxes, their battles had been incessant and indecisive. Just as one

Canada geese and their family.

gander was gaining mastery over the next most powerful contender, he was carried away by success as he and his goose chased their rival to the other end of the pool.

Carrion crows are the opportunists of the feathered world, and a black old villain had been waiting patiently for just such a turn-up for the book. Without an instant's hesitation, he nipped in and scoffed the eggs in the nest that the triumphant pair had temporarily vacated. The poor old goose set to and laid another clutch, but the raiders returned and scoffed all but five of the eggs out of that nest too.

That was a week ago and after four long weeks of patient incubation, the goose appeared on the pool with 100 per cent hatch of five goslings. I watched them through my field glasses with interest but without enthusiasm.

Last year I had tried to get a good crop of water weed to grow in the pool so that it would attract water insects which, in turn, would attract dab chicks and other delightful waterfowl. I sowed an acre or so of grass seed in a clearing I had made at the edge of the pool. Neither project was very successful. Before either the weed or the grass got going, we had an invasion of more than twenty Canada geese which pulled up the water weeds before they got established, and nipped off the young grass as efficiently as gallons of weed killer. Canada geese were not my favourite birds.

It was really my admiration for the pugnacity of this year's gander, who has kept most of his rivals away, that induced me to tolerate his presence. But he would have been more welcome if his goose had hatched two instead of five!

When my powerful glasses brought his fluffy goslings into sharp focus, apparently only a few yards away, I had to admit that whoever failed to fall under their spell must have a heart of stone. As soon as her goslings were dry after hatching from the egg, the goose had led them on to the water which is where I first caught sight of them. They floated on the pool, buoyant as corks and soft as the down that clothed them. Within half an hour, she led them to the banks so that they could start to graze. There is a belt of rough reeds around the edge of the pool which must look like scaling a mountain to anything as tiny as a young goose. Four of the brood got up as easily as if they had practised for weeks. The fifth stayed on the water.

The goose, gander and four who were prepared to conform went to a patch of tender turf about five yards from the edge. The little rebel stayed and yelled his head off. Then he fell on his back and lay vainly struggling in the sticky mud. The gander walked back to survey the extent of the catastrophe and apparently told the stupid creature to pull himself together and get out.

The helpless gosling was stuck so fast that he would obviously have died and I was tempted to go to the rescue but, not suffering fools gladly, I hung on to see what happened. The gander jumped down beside his offspring and gave him such a savage peck that he flicked him into the air and he landed right way up. Chastened, the gosling climbed the proper way up the bank and joined his mates in a feast of succulent grass.

At dusk, the goose led the way back to the edge, and swam over to the island to spend the night in safety and – you've guessed – only four goslings joined her.

Remembering his experience in the mud, the fifth funked it in spite of cajoling and threats from his parents. So, on the principle that the weak must be cosseted, the whole family returned and joined him.

I don't know what happened during the hours of darkness. Perhaps Charlie Fox paid them a visit or a rat or a stoat. When I looked out of the window at first light, the whole family had settled, safe from disturbance, on the island where they were hatched. Well, not quite the whole family. One was missing. The wise old birds must have decided it was not reasonable to put the fate of their four well-disciplined young at peril for the sake of a silly drop-out.

55.   An Indomitable Rabbit

Bunz doesn't know how lucky he is. By all the rules, he should be dead. Paul Lowe was going home in the small hours after a party last July when he noticed a brown bundle of fur scuffling helplessly around in the middle of the road. Stopping the car, he found that some previous driver had hit a young rabbit and left it there to die. One eye was closed right up, it was covered in blood and apparently unconscious although its reflexes were still impelling the series of convulsions which had first attracted Paul's attention.

Most people would have passed by on the other side, or I suppose practical countrymen might have knocked him on the head to put him out of his misery.

Paul's first impulse was to find a vet but all the local vets were tucked up, enjoying their beauty sleep and he didn't reckon they would relish being dragged out of bed to a casualty rabbit.

So he took it home.

Mrs Lowe, his mother, also has an incurably soft heart. Together they sponged the victim clean, moistened his lips with milk and water and laid him gently in a cardboard box. Neither of them reckoned that Bunz had any chance of survival but they felt that the least they could do was to ensure that he had a comfortable and dignified end. Paul took the cardboard box to bed with him in case the patient needed anything in the night.

Next morning, he hadn't moved and was still unconscious. So they moistened his lips and left him to sleep himself away.

Three days later, he was still out to the world but his spark of life continued to smoulder. The will to live and sheer tenacity of life in such weaklings is often incredible. On the fourth morning, when Paul looked in the box, there was nothing there. Young Bunz was belting round under the bed as if he had a whippet after his scut.

Since that day, he has never looked back. Wild rabbits are often practically untamable but Bunz settled in as one of the family. The problem was – where to put him?

Mrs Lowe disagrees, as I do, with importing tortoises as pets for so many die because of ignorance and neglect (see No. 12 on page 44). So her incurable heart impelled her to fence off about a third of her garden as a refuge for waif and stray tortoises. The tortoise sanctuary seemed the ideal place for Bunz to share as it has shrubs, grass, lettuce and dandelion, and dry, warm sheds for shelter. The snag was that every household in the area seemed to harbour about two cats per head of indigenous population. And cats are even more dangerous to young rabbits than late-night motorists.

So the Lowes heightened the fence round the tortoise sanctuary, topping it with plastic sheets which they hoped would give no foothold for cats. Such man-made fortifications are treated with scorn by gang-ster moggies so that Bunz is brought indoors at night, for his own safety. And, I might add, because the whole Lowe family dote on his company!

He has dishes of rabbit food which he spurns because he thinks that only common rabbits would eat it. But he likes Wensleydale cheese and granary bread and a little cooked parsnip, with butter, as a nightcap. He likes a little dried fruit and nuts, but he is so finicky that he hasn't grown as he should – and that is how I came to be introduced.

He is a rangy, leggy rabbit so that, although they called him Bunz, Mrs Lowe began to wonder if he was really a hare, and invited me over to meet him. Although I have been a ferreting man all my life, he showed not the slightest fear of me and, although his colour is a bit sandy for a rabbit, I was able to confirm that his blood bore no trace of hare.

He stays with the family and the spaniel and the rescued, retired greyhound all evening, and never blots his copybook by spending a penny on the carpet. When he gets restless, Mrs Lowe carries him up to the tortoise sanctuary (whatever the weather) and he empties himself in only one specific corner. In the snow, he would wait patiently for it to be cleared before he sought relief.

Then he is returned to the sitting-room for the rest of the evening and bites playfully – but quite hard – if there is any attempt to put him to bed before he is ready. At last he suffers himself to be wrapped in a warm blanket and carried up to Paul's room where he spends the night, never leaving the tiniest puddle or smell.

Even I, who have the traditional countryman's reserve about rabbits, am bound to admit that he is, in every way, a charmer. But, as I said, I don't think he knows how very lucky he is.

56. Sixth Sense

Tick knows when I have got out of bed the wrong side long before she sees me. She sleeps in the kitchen and, when she hears me coming down stairs, nips out of her box and grabs a towel and oven glove from the rail behind the door. She is adept at wrapping them up and by the time I open the door, she has them both rolled into a neat ball which she offers me as a present the moment we meet.

She is so delighted to see me that her whole body wags in ecstasy and it is impossible not to be infected by her enthusiasm. Or almost impossible.

Just occasionally, when my temper happens to be a bit frayed at the edges, I am in no mood to be met by such an effusive display and her gift gets rather a bore. If I don't make much of her and tell her what a generous dog she is, she is mortally offended and sulks for the rest of the morning.

This rarely happens now because, if I am not disposed to form a mutual admiration society with her, she seems to know by instinct. When I am feeling out of sorts, there is no wrapped-up present to greet me and I find her lying in her bed with a hurt look in her eyes, showing no sign that she is pleased to see me.

I have no idea how she is able to sense my mood even before I put my nose round the kitchen door. Perhaps I descend the stairs with a heavy tread which is her warning that I shall be churlish about her advances. I certainly neither sing nor whistle when I'm cheerful so I cannot think of any obvious clue she may pick up.

I have a hunch that our sub-conscious communication goes far deeper than that.

If I have been away all day, and the dogs are snoozing by the fire, my wife says Tick gets restless two or three minutes before I arrive. I am no slouch when driving so I must then be much too far from home for even the most sensitive ears to pick up the sound of my engine and, as I don't return at the same time two days running, it would not help if she understood the clock.

173

Sceptics might say it is all a matter of acute observation and there is no doubt that Tick and Belle are no fools at noticing the clues and putting two and two together. They are inveterate eavesdroppers and evidently listen in to our conversation. For most of the time it must be double Dutch to them but they latch on immediately to words and phrases that concern them.

'Going round the wood' or 'feed the stock' or 'see if there is anything about' in the most conversational tone have them standing quivering with anticipation that they will be invited to join in.

There are several badger setts in the woods and the dogs know they are never allowed near them, although I doubt if they appreciate the reason. I won't risk alien scents disturbing the occupants.

Past experience has taught them that I make them lie down and wait some yards away before I approach a sett to examine it. But I often find

Tick seems to have a sixth sense.

they do not wait for my verbal command. They seem able to steal the thought from the back of my mind for, the instant I *think* about telling them to lie down, they anticipate the command and comply before I have had time to translate the thought into words.

They have a similar close mental link between themselves. Belle may be fifty yards away, out of sight behind a clump of dense cover, but she is still able to sense Tick's excitement. Time after time I have seen her stop dead in her tracks, head held high to see, hear or smell the cause of Tick's interest. Then she will leave whatever she is doing and rush over to the old bitch, eager to share the discovery.

There is no doubt in my mind that dogs have some sensitive sixth sense which we seem to have lost in the course of civilisation.

57.   The Price Of Over-Eating

The bird box by my study window has always been a great success. Blue tits breed in it every year and, although this year's brood is a little late because of the weather, the old birds started feeding about a week ago.

They would have been about half-grown when my wife noticed a weasel climbing the wooden fencing pole to which I had screwed the box. She flung open the window and poured maledictions on his head so that, not surprisingly, he reckoned the odds were against him and did a bunk.

After that, everything went normally until I noticed the cock bird standing on the roof of the box, peering cautiously over and chattering with rage. It was an uncharacteristic attitude as he had spent the last few days flying fearlessly in and out in his constant efforts to cram his insatiable chicks with juicy caterpillars.

As I watched him, it became obvious that something serious was wrong and I remembered the weasel my wife had chivvied away. When I got near enough to squint into the nesting I was greeted by an overpowering pong of musk and a furious chattering that I recognised as a weasel's foulest language. He had evidently returned when no one was about, to complete the wretched slaughter my wife thought she had prevented.

I had constructed the box very carefully. It was eight inches high, with a sloping roof and the sides were six inches square. The only entrance was through a circular hole precisely one inch and a sixteenth across, which allows blue tits to creep through but is too small sor sparrows and larger birds.

Unfortunately, it also proved to be just large enough for a weasel to squeeze through. He must have clambered up the pole and poked his head into the hole to do a macabre stock-taking of the contents of the box. If he had come at dusk or dawn, the hen bird would probably have been there brooding her chicks.

The temptation must have been irresistible. Once his head was

A weasel peering out to check that the coast is clear.

through the hole, the old bird and her chicks would scream and fluster in panic, enticing him to supreme efforts. Gradually his sinuous body would inch itself through the hole while the mother hen pecked and battered him with her puny wings. When he heaved his back legs through the hole, he would have been free to retaliate by savaging the hen bird and then her chicks.

That is what I believed to have happened. What I am certain about is that, when I went outside, the box contained a weasel who was very cross indeed, partly because I had caught him in the act and partly because the hole, which had been only just big enough to allow him to squeeze through, was now too small to allow him to squeeze out again. Or, to be more precise, he was now too big to squeeze out! His four-star meal of a hen blue it and anything up to ten fledglings had swelled his belly until it wouldn't go through the exit.

I had to get the roof off to get him out, and it faced me with the problem of what I should do with him. Blue tits are a natural item of diet for weasels and the hunter had obviously done nothing 'wrong'. But if I let him go, the chances were that he would be hooked on small birds as easy and tasty prey to catch so that he would almost certainly have cleaned out all the other broods in my nest boxes round the wood as well as any other nests where he heard young calling for food.

So I gave him no more chance than a gamekeeper would have done if he had caught him in his pheasant-rearing pens. It went against the grain with me, partly because I have had two marvellously tame weasels which were among the most delightful creatures I have ever been associated with.

I occasionally catch a stoat raiding my fowl pen, or a fox that gets similar ideas – and I never feel happy about that either. To some extent, I think, there are 'rogues' among animals as there are with us. Not, of course, in the sense of bad characters, but certainly some animals behave differently from the normal behaviour of their species.

Weasels, for instance, usually prefer furred, when they can get it, to feathered prey. The rough ground around the garden teems with fieldmice and voles and the weasels follow them in and normally keep their numbers down to a level where my wife can grow peas and beans and cherished flowers. When there are plenty of voles, the weasels don't normally seem to bother the birds much so that we are delighted to welcome them.

In the same way, when there are plenty of rabbits about, as there are at present, the foxes use them as staple diet and rarely raid my poultry or even the pheasants who nest in the wood.

Rats are the one species which are never welcome. I trap them, ferret them and catch them with the dogs at night. I gas them and poison them and kill them any way I can, but they never heed the warning that there is no welcome on my mat.

58.   Delightful Downpour

Having spent three steamy days sweating it out at the Game Fair, the sudden deluge last Sunday was more welcome than a draught of champagne. It came as a pleasant surprise, for I had just prodded myself into action and run out 100 yards of hose to save the life of a great clump of rhododendrons that fills a gap between the garden and the drive.

The flies were flaying me alive and I mistook the first few drops for midges which had come to reinforce the attack of the bigger buzzing bullies, and I tried to brush them off.

Bad news dawns at once, but it is astonishing how dense one can be to appreciate when things are going right. It wasn't until the evidence of my ears confirmed that it was really beginning to rain, in thunderous drops large enough to play the soft, rhythmic percussion that refreshes parched ground, that I tumbled to the fact that a welcome change had arrived.

When I had returned home the previous night, the first thing I had done was to wallow in a hot bath to flush out the fine Wiltshire dust that had caked all over me as effectively as a crust of pastry, but soapy water is never really satisfying. The cool deluge was instantly refreshing and I stood out in it, allowing it to drench me to the skin. I never really appreciate how delicious rain can be until it comes at the end of a hot and sticky spell.

I was not alone in appreciating it. In front of my study window, there is a large bird bath which I clean and fill every morning when I feed the stock. There is a constant procession to drink and bathe all day, and the most enthusiastic of all my customers are the pouter pigeons whose desire for personal hygiene would leave the theatre sister at any hospital far behind. Having a natural aversion to drinking their own bath water, they dip in their bills, and suck great draughts to quench their thirst.

None of your dainty dipping the tip of their beak into the water and tipping their heads up for them. Pigeons stick their bills right in and suck the stuff down as vigorously as horses. Only when they have quenched their thirst do they get around to their ablutions. Then they wade in, high up their long thighs and shake their feathers as vigorously as belly dancers so that wave after wave is sluiced right down to their skin.

It is efficient and obviously pleasurable – but like most good things in life, it takes a lot of effort so they were not slow to take advantage of the unexpected thunderstorm. On the roof of the outbuilding, the whole flock lined up, all facing the same way, with one wing outstretched so that the underside was exposed to the sky. It may sound ridiculous to suggest that pigeons can be expressive. But I am certain that their look of smug satisfaction was no figment of my imagination.

And why should they not have been pleased with themselves? There they sat, having to make not the slightest effort, while the coolest, cleanest shower was apparently laid on especially for them. As soon as one wing was cooled, they closed it and turned so that the other wing was exposed and the dose was repeated. No gaggle of beauties sun-bathing on some expensive foreign beach ever looked more self-satisfied.

Meanwhile, the deer came out of the dense thickets where they had been vainly trying to shelter from the flies. Such great drops of rain do not seem to annihilate tiny midges because each raindrop pushes before it a cushion of air which acts as a buffer to shove very small insects out of the way before the water can hit them. But larger flies, the sort that torment deer, do not like heavy rain and take shelter until it is over.

The deer came out and immediately began to graze. Although their pasture is sweet and rich in clover, the long, dry spell had made it as dry and dusty as canteen cakes. They ripped off the newly washed herbage as if it were their first feed after a hard winter and all that was to be seen on their coats were raindrops as large as bluebottles but not as aggravating.

Deer are particularly choosy about what rain they will tolerate. They hate the unpredictable splashes that fall from trees when wet eventually seeps through the branches and falls to the woodland floor. Deer would far rather stand in the open and take all that a downpour offers.

Watching them feeding in the storm the other day, it was easy to see why. Most of the water simply slid off as smooth as the proverbial water off a duck's back. But, every now and then, they shook their skins so vigorously that a cascade of tiny droplets simply showered off them. It was as efficient as being rubbed down with the finest towel.

They say 1976 was the Year of the Ladybird and there is no doubt that the previous year or so had caused a population explosion. This year may well go down as the Year of the Greenfly. Motorists in many parts were literally stopped by hordes of greenflies which coated their windscreens. We have had them in the garden and one favourite bird cherry tree was so coated that my wife despaired for it. Nature's way of dealing with such plagues is as efficient as chemical pesticides – and far less dangerous.

The heavy rain which delighted the pigeons, the deer and me, was too much for the greenflies. It torrented over the leaves of the afflicted tree and sluiced them off to the ground below where they struggled round as helpless as if they had been brewed into soup.

That evening, when I took the dogs out for a walk in the cool clean air, the grass was alive with toads which come down to the pool to breed each spring, and hibernate several hundred yards away. I knew they had left the pool, but I had not seen any during the dry spell. They need water to keep their skins moist and, in dry weather, they cower under shaded roots and stones. The wet had brought them out, too, and they had found the greenfly. I was delighted to see them gorging on the pests and putting an end to their prosperity.

59.   Out-Foxed

As a naturalist, I take a keen interest in the habits of creatures around me. And I like to think I am objective, getting neither sentimental nor excited about the dramas I often see.

It does not always work like that. The late spring and dry spell we have had recently have allowed the laying hens to scratch the top off the enclosure where there is usually enough green grass to keep them more than happy. So I threw open the gate between the spinney and their paddock and allowed them to wander.

You have never seen more happy hens. They spent the first few days working around the edge of the pool, where they found enough slugs and beetles to give a wonderful flavour to their eggs.

Within a few days, they gradually ventured further into the wood, evidently discovering plenty of tasty treasures in the leaf mould. I did wonder about foxes but the game cock is a vigilant old fellow and I trusted him to give his hens sufficient warning to flee for safety. We have quite a few rabbits about this year and hunting men will tell you that foxes will not cause much damage while they have no difficulty in supplying their menu with rabbits.

There is more than a grain of truth in this because to 'breed like rabbits' is no exaggeration and our rabbit population seems about static, so that something must be keeping them in check. There is an old saying that claims:

> Big fleas have little fleas
> Upon their backs to bite them,
> Little fleas have lesser fleas
> And so ad infinitum.

This is certainly true where I am concerned. We had a litter of foxes in a stick pile, up the wood, so I mentioned it to Tom, the gamekeeper on the land adjoining mine. I did not get on with the last keeper who I believed, rightly or wrongly, harried my badgers 'when they strayed on to his beat'. But Tom is different. He is ultra-careful not to harm the badgers which both of us believe are virtually harmless to game.

In exchange, I am quite happy for him to come into my wood to drive back home any pheasants that he has reared, or to thin out the carrion crows and other vermin that put his work at risk.

Tom doesn't like foxes. One fox among newly-released pheasants can spell disaster to months of his hard work. So, when I told him about the litter of cubs in the wood, he was round within five minutes. He brought Andy, his assistant, and a chap who was fencing in my wood, but is widely known as a crack shot.

They put a terrier down the hole and, before they had time to cock their guns, the vixen and two cubs had bolted for safety. Needless to say, they went out where the crack shot was waiting – and he missed the lot! So I got the blame for employing him! We saw nothing of those foxes for weeks. Their narrow squeak had convinced them that there

A fine fox watching keenly for the slightest sign of a potential victim.

are less risky places to live than in my wood.

When my hens started to wander further afield, I was relieved the foxes had been scared off first. Then one day last week I was sitting at my desk, gazing into space for some inspiration, when a movement caught my attention. There was an explosion among a group of four rabbits that had been quietly grazing for the last half hour. And, right into the middle of where they had been, stood a magnificent russet fox cub. He was physically well-grown but his technique obviously had a long way to go. Those rabbits simply made rings around him.

That was in broad daylight, about half past nine in the morning. Foxes being creatures of habit, I kept my eyes skinned about the same time the next day. Failure had apparently disheartened him because I saw no more signs – until today.

Just as I sat down to decide what to write about, there was another explosion. It was not among the rabbits this time, but among my laying hens. They were scratching about, right out in the open, when the russet bombshell landed in their midst. Domestic hens are not as agile as wild rabbits and, when the cloud of feathers subsided, one hen was missing. It made a gallant try to escape, somersaulting the cub several times, but all in vain. He kept grip, shook the life out of it and made off into the wood before I could unhook my rifle from the stand.

I hope he doesn't know the rhyme about the fleas because next time he comes, he will find me waiting and, when it is *my* hens I am protecting, I am not a bad shot!

60.   Boffins Or Buffoons?

For sheer stupidity, the British Farm Produce Council must surely be in a class of their own. It has seriously listed the wren as a 'natural enemy' of the trout, although it graciously says that it is not ásking for action against wrens to be taken 'at the moment'.

Wrens are among our smallest birds (only two species are smaller) and they live on insects, spiders and other minute live food. They have suffered particularly badly during the last winter because their bodies are so small they are incapable of retaining enough body heat to survive long winter nights without artificial aid.

But the tiny birds have an instinct to huddle together in communal roosts on frosty nights, so their combined warmth keeps them alive until morning. The less their numbers grow, the less chance the dwindling number of survivors have of living to see the dawn. When the weather is not cold, they are territorial and pugnacious little birds, so they are never very thick on the ground.

As each weighs only a fraction of an ounce, their impact on trout fry (or young) can only be so small as to be negligible. Among other 'enemies' of their beloved trout, the Council has listed blackbirds which they accuse of sweeping over the water like seagulls! If they ever took time off to go to the seaside, they would soon see that seagulls do no damage to fish while they are sweeping over the water. The time when the fish need to look after their skins is when the gulls stop sweeping over the water and take a dip with the fish.

Blackbirds, in case the British Farm Produce Council have not noticed, do not have webbed feet nor do they swim after their prey!

But sportsmen, and sometimes farmers, have a habit of giving themselves a deplorable public image by demanding the extinction of any creature they believe could cause the slightest harm to their interest even if, as in this case, the whole thing is such obvious nonsense.

The British Farm Produce Council, however, have really excelled themselves. Wrens are alleged to wreak havoc because they are so tiny they can creep through the netting the fish farmers pull over their tanks of young fish. Blackbirds can sweep about as much as they like, but presumably they will not be able to penetrate the defences, quite apart from the fact that they couldn't do any serious damage if they did.

'Serious', of course, is the operative word. My view is that there is ample room for all sorts of interest in the countryside provided there is reasonable give and take. The real troubles start when one interest – be it sporting, farming or conservation – claims the right to obliterate everything that might interfere with its interests in the slightest.

A friend of mine recently heard a fish farm manager boasting that he had shot several kingfishers for poaching his young trout. Kingfishers are on the Schedule of Protected Birds, but what goes on in the privacy of an isolated fish farm is very hard to prove. But it may be significant that the British Farm Produce Council also nominates kingfishers as 'natural enemies' of trout, along with herons and wrens.

A wren brings food back to the nest for its young.

So far as I can see, they don't mention otters, which could certainly do more damage than either, but otters are such a sensitive subject that it may be that they are quietly knocked off without making a song about it.

In any case, if fishermen can afford a couple of hundred pounds a year to fish reservoirs – the going rate in the Midlands – and far more in rivers where the sport is really good, it is a pity if they can't afford to rear a few extra trout for the wrens and otters and kingfishers.

A great deal of havoc to wildlife is caused not so much by people like the fish farmers themselves but by their customers who, presumably, don't know any better. No vandals leave more litter about than some fishermen after a day's sport. (See No. 24 on page 78). A recent report by a section of the British Trust for Ornithology revealed that over five and a half miles of fishing line had been found alongside the banks of the river examined. It is diabolical stuff; it entangles birds and small animals and does nothing for the digestion of farm stock grazing there. Birds of seventeen species, ranging from tiny swifts to huge swans, were found dead, entangled by discarded fishing line.

They also found over three thousand pieces of lead shot, which birds mistake for grit which they need to grind their food when it reaches the gizzard.

In addition, every reservoir and river bank has its quota of broken bottles to cut cattle's feet, and plastic bags to clog up their insides.

The British Farm Produce Council must not persist in talking rubbish about wrens, kingfishers and herons being 'natural enemies' of fish farmers . . . implying the poor fish farmers will not be able to line their pockets if they are not allowed to exterminate any wildlife they do not like. If they don't desist, they may find that conservationists will not be slow to take a leaf out of their book and 'ask for action to be taken against fish farmers'.

They do not share with wrens the privilege of being covered by the Protection of Birds Act.

Index